# Perspectives on History

# Perspectives on History

William Dray

**ROUTLEDGE & KEGAN PAUL**
London, Boston and Henley

First published in 1980
by Routledge & Kegan Paul Ltd
39 Store Street, London WC1E 7DD,
9 Park Street, Boston, Mass. 02108, USA and
Broadway House, Newtown Road,
Henley-on-Thames, Oxon RG9 1EN and
Set in 10/11pt Times by
Hope Services, Abingdon, Oxon
and printed in Great Britain by
Redwood Burn Ltd
Trowbridge & Esher
© William Dray, 1980

British Library Cataloguing in Publication Data

Dray, William

Perspectives on history.
1. Historiography – Addresses, essays, lectures
2. History – Philosophy – Addresses, essays,
lectures
I. Title
907'.2        D13        79-42651

ISBN 0 7100 0569 5
ISBN 0 7100 0570 9 Pbk

To friends at Trent

# Contents

# Acknowledgments

The chapter on Collingwood appeared in a slightly different French version under the title 'R.G. Collingwood et la connaissance historique', in *Dialogue*, 17: 4, 1978, pp. 659–82, and is reprinted by permission of the Editors of *Dialogue* and the Officers of the Canadian Philosophical Association. The chapters on Watkins and Spengler use some material from my articles, 'Holism and Individualism in History and the Social Sciences' and 'Oswald Spengler', in Paul Edwards, Editor-in-Chief, *The Encyclopedia of Philosophy*, New York, Free Press, 1967, vol. 4, pp. 53–8 and vol. 7, pp. 527–30 respectively, Copyright © 1967 by Macmillan, Inc. The chapter on Taylor, without the concluding section, was published in almost identical form under the title, 'Concepts of Causation in A.J.P. Taylor's Account of the Origins of the Second World War', in *History and Theory*, 17: 2, 1978, pp. 149–74, Copyright 1978 by Wesleyan University. I am grateful for permissions to reprint or draw upon these previously published writings. I should like also to express my thanks to the members of the Department of Philosophy at Trent for their kind invitation to give the lectures, and their encouragement with regard to their publication, as well as to colleagues who cast a critical eye over the manuscript before its final submission.

Acknowledgments

# Introduction

This book is composed of papers written at various times for various purposes. Versions of four of them were delivered at Trent University, Peterborough, Canada, in March 1978, as the Gilbert Ryle Lectures, Second Series, and a fifth was read to the Champlain Society at Trent during the same period. The purpose of the lectures was to introduce audiences consisting mainly of students of philosophy and history to some of the main concerns of contemporary philosophy of history, in Great Britain and North America. In their present emended form they offer 'perspectives' on the subject from a number of points of view.

The three chapters of Part One deal in turn with three of the problems that have been most frequently discussed in recent so-called critical philosophy of history:[1] the nature of historical understanding, the extent to which historians can attain objectivity, and the relation of individual human agents and social groups in historical thinking. The approach to the problem in each case is through an analysis of views of a well-known author. On the problem of understanding, the chosen author is R.G. Collingwood, the Oxford philosopher, historian and archaeologist, who, in the years between the World Wars, first made the examination of history as a special form of knowledge a live issue in English philosophy. On the problem of objectivity, the position discussed in that of Charles Beard, the American revisionist historian, who, under the influence of Croce and other European philosophers in the 1930s, did more than most to heighten the methodological self-consciousness of the historical profession in the United States. On the problem of individual and group, the view considered is that of J.W.N. Watkins, a contemporary philosopher of the social sciences at the London School of Economics, whose writings in that wider field, largely inspired by ideas of F.A. von Hayek and K.R. Popper,

1

have always shown a special sensitivity to the concerns and problems of historical inquiry.

Approaching the problems through a somewhat detailed critique of certain contentions of selected authors, rather than discussing them directly, necessarily entails, of course, some loss of comprehensiveness in the consideration of the problems themselves. This is especially true in the case of Collingwood, where the focus will be on a single controversial claim of his about historical understanding. However, for purposes of introducing readers to the subject, there are compensating advantages in focusing on views of authors whose doctrines have been given serious consideration in recent discussion. References in the notes offer some guidance for further reading in each case.

Part Two is also concerned with a central problem of critical philosophy of history. This is the problem of the nature of causal judgment in the sorts of inquiries historians undertake, with special reference to the distinction they commonly draw between true causes and relevant, but non-causal 'background' conditions. However, the approach taken to this problem is very different from that taken to the problems dealt with in Part One. What is examined in the three chapters of Part One is certain philosophical theories bearing on the particular problems posed: theories which, if sound, would, it is certainly to be hoped, throw some light on the practice of historians. What is examined in Part Two, by contrast, is an actual example of historical practice, with a view to elaborating a philosophical theory about it. The example selected is a celebrated controversy between the English historian, A.J.P. Taylor, and some of his critics, over the causes of the Second World War. This controversy has the advantage, for present purposes, not only of offering an abundance of explicit argument, laced with occasional theoretical observations on the part of the historians involved, but also of being readily accessible for further study both in Taylor's *Origins of the Second World War*.[2] and in various anthologies collecting responses to it. Two of the latter are referred to in the notes to chapter IV.

The inclusion, in a rather brief introductory book, of a philosophical analysis of a fairly lengthy sample of actual historical argument — an approach to the problems of philosophy of history, as it were, from the bottom up rather than from the top down — is not accidental or unmotivated. What analytical philosophers, in particular, have had to say about history in recent years, although it has attained a considerable level of sophistication and elegance, has increasingly come under fire from historians themselves as being irrelevant to what they actually do. Thus Geoffrey Elton in his *Political History*,[3] after ironically expressing wonder at the ability of philosophers to 'to argue logically about abstractions', deplores their 'apparent ignorance of what actually happens when an historian investigates the past'. Nowhere is this more evident, he says, than in their 'persistent failure to choose sound examples', these too often being derived from 'higher-flown think-pieces about the meaning of history to which some historians are prone', or, even more likely, 'general works' which convey the results of historical thinking, if at all, only at second hand. I am myself accused of having once based a whole philosophical argument on a citation from such a secondary source, in which the historian was just 'using a phrase he had not thought through in order to end a paragraph'. J.H. Hexter has expressed his dissatisfaction with recent philosophy of history in similar terms. In a section of his *History Primer*[4] ominously entitled 'Obstacles to Understanding History', he, too, warns of 'illusions' about the subject fostered by 'all sorts of Deep Thinkers', but mainly philosophers. For 'even when actual historical writing was presumably the substance with which the philosophers were concerned', he complains, 'they often seemed to abstract so ruthlessly from the actual structure of such writing and to so atomize it as to destroy the sense of its integrity as a significant form of discourse.'

Not everything in this chorus of disapproval from both sides of the Atlantic is equally deserving of the philosopher of history's attention. For example, the very nature of his inquiry surely requires a philosopher to abstract. His task is not simply to describe procedures of historical research: it is to elicit structures characterizing historical thought, and to elaborate theories about them. Nor should the warning against historians' 'think-pieces' be allowed to obscure the fact that much is to be learned from attending to the theoretical reflections of historians — including, it might be added, those of Elton and Hexter.[5] This is, in fact, true even of some of the 'higher-flown' variety: for example, those of Beard, whose writings, discussed in Part One of this book, might well be thought, by some of his less venturesome professional colleagues, to fall into this category.

There is nevertheless some justice in the complaint that even philosophers who would claim relevance to actual historical inquiry for their theoretical investigations (and not all would[6]), have offered too few analyses of fairly extensive examples of historical work. It is therefore to be hoped that what is offered in Part Two of this book may be considered, by those who make such criticism, as a step in the right direction. It is to be hoped, also, that it may make clearer to any historians who read it, the kind of *interest* that critical philosophers have in their discipline, and how this meshes with their own. Not that a philosopher will ever carry the judgment of all historians in his selection of materials for analysis. Indeed, it is unlikely that either Elton or Hexter would entirely approve of my choice of the Taylor controversy.[7] It is not even clear that Taylor and his chief critic, H.R. Trevor-Roper, to judge from the tone of some of their exchanges, would consider each other's work as affording suitable data for philosophical theorizing. Clearly, the philosopher must sometimes be prepared simply to take a risk in this regard.

There is another kind of reservation that might perhaps be felt, at any rate by Elton, about the present attempt to make contact with historical practice. This is that, although a certain amount of historical 'writing' is reviewed, the analysis offered does not address itself directly to the problem of 'what actually happens when an historian investigates the past'. Its concern, it might be objected, is more that of a consumer than that of a producer of historical accounts: its central question is how the conclusions and supporting arguments of historians are legitimately to be *understood*. To ask the latter sort of question, however, is surely *one* crucial aspect of any philosophical critique of a discipline. If arguments of the sort mounted by Taylor and his critics do not tell us anything about the nature and status of historians' knowledge-claims about the past, it is difficult to see what would. In fact, it is not easy to maintain a sharp distinction between historical 'inquiry' and historical 'writing' — which seems to be Elton's intent. The point is one on which he and Hexter seem not themselves to be entirely in agreement, the latter being more inclined to ask how well philosophers have come to grips with what historians 'write'.

In Part Three, I turn from the concern of critical philosophy with the concepts and structures of argument that characterize history as a type of inquiry or a mode of knowledge to look at an example of philosophy of history in a more traditional, and perhaps more popular, sense. This is the account of what is most significant about the course of world history, considered as a whole, given by the German author, Oswald Spengler, in his monumental work, *The Decline of the West.*[8] Philosophical interpretations of history, understood as the course of events rather than as a type of inquiry into it, have generally been referred to, in the English-speaking world, as 'speculative' philosophy of history. This terminology is not entirely appropriate; for although most philosophical interpretations of the historical process itself, from nineteenth-century figures like Hegel, Comte, and even Marx, all the way back to cyclical theorists among the ancient Greek philosophers, have, in fact, been highly speculative, the essential difference is not really one of methods or standards, but of subject-matter or questions asked. It must nevertheless be said, and it is argued below, that Spengler's dazzling account of history as a whole is indeed highly speculative; and it may well be that a close scrutiny of even one such interpretive system will convince most readers that the enterprise itself would always be so.

What is illustrative of contemporary British and American phil-

4

osophy of history is not, of course, Spengler's system, or even the concerns which drive him to construct it — English thought not, in fact, having been particularly productive of such systems, or particularly responsive to such concerns. It is rather the kind of critique to which it is subjected, which amounts to a kind of critical philosophy of a speculative philosophy of history. If some readers, as they proceed, feel that the critique is rather a long time coming, my excuse must be the following. First, since what is at issue is the *system* — the way the various ideas, some of them initially quite obscure, fit together to provide a plausible way of regarding history as a whole — a rather higher proportion of chapter V than of the others is devoted to sheer exposition of the selected author's doctrines. Second, whether or not one is prepared, in the end, actually to accept a speculative philosophy of history like Spengler's, many will see it as intrinsically interesting to explore such intellectual constructions in some detail, if only to see them as ways in which one might be *tempted* to regard the human past. It seems to me that, from this point of view at least, Spengler's views are more interesting than most.

I have nevertheless taken it for granted that, no matter how Spengler himself may seem, at times, implicitly to reject such an approach to his work, his account of the significance of world history is to be judged, in the end, both by the coherence of its system of ideas and by the degree to which its claims can be appropriately grounded in ascertainable historical fact (what exactly 'appropriately' means here remaining to be seen). That is, I have assumed that what Spengler offers us is, to some important degree, an empirical hypothesis, this making it both more vulnerable, and also more worth considering, than most of the speculative systems of the past. In this respect, as well as many others, it resembles the account of world history given by his near-contemporary, Arnold Toynbee, the only English speculative philosopher of history of any stature.[9] In considering Spengler's views, I have therefore, from time to time, called attention to contrasts and comparisons between the two. And since Spengler's defenders sometimes half-justify his account as, at any rate, conveying an authentic 'personal vision' of the past, I have included also, as I did not in the case of the other authors, a little information about Spengler the man, and the circumstances under which his ideas were formed and advanced.

# Part One

# I R.G. Collingwood and the Understanding of Actions in History

## I

Any attempt to come to grips with contemporary discussion of history by English-speaking philosophers must take account, at some point, of the views of R.G. Collingwood. Ever since the appearance in 1946 of his posthumous monograph, *The Idea of History*,[1] Collingwood's doctrines have been a widely-acknowledged stimulus to both philosophers and historians concerned to characterize history as a type of inquiry or mode of knowledge. And since the publication in 1962 of Alan Donagan's path-breaking study, *The Later Philosophy of R.G. Collingwood*,[2] a growing exegetical and critical literature on his writings has made his claims about history the harder to ignore. In what follows, my aim will be to clarify and discuss what I take to be one of Collingwood's central contentions. This is that the understanding of the past in a properly historical way requires, on the part of the historian, a *re-enactment of past experience* or a *re-thinking of past thought*.

Perhaps no doctrine of Collingwood's has generated more opposition. Much of the criticism it has received, however, has centred less upon the legitimacy of the notion itself than upon its alleged narrowness as a *general* account of historical understanding. It has been argued that, even if historians, on occasion, re-enact the experience or re-think the thoughts of past agents, the kind of understanding this yields would be relevant to only a small fraction of history's normal concerns. Collingwood's account has been held to be inapplicable to the explanation of social processes; to ignore the role of the natural environment in human affairs; and even in the case of individual human experience, to put a premium quite arbitrarily on certain restricted forms of it, namely on what is self-conscious, thoughtful and rational.[3]

Difficulties of these kinds seem to me often in fact to have been exaggerated; and I shall give some reasons for holding this to be the case. The focus of what I want to say, however, will be less on the problem of the scope of Collingwood's doctrine than on the prior question of how it, and some associated claims, should be understood where they *do* apply, notably to the attempt to understand a single action of a single historical agent. I shall begin with a consideration of the way Collingwood originally presents his view of understanding, and then go on to discuss some problems often thought to arise for its application even to this, its most favourable case.

## II

The best short statement of Collingwood's theory of understanding in history is given in three or four pages of the section of *The Idea of History* entitled 'Human Nature and Human History', a section which may be regarded as having particular authority since, unlike most of the book, it was published during the author's lifetime, after being read to the British Academy in 1936. The main drift of Collingwood's account there could be summarized as follows, largely in his own words.[4]

'The historian, investigating any event in the past, makes a distinction between what may be called the outside and the inside of an event.' By the outside is meant 'everything belonging to it which can be described in terms of bodies and their movements'; for example, 'the passage of Caesar, accompanied by certain men, across a river called the Rubicon' at a certain date. By the inside is meant 'that in it which can only be described in terms of thought'; for example, 'Caesar's defiance of Republican law'. The historian 'is never concerned with either of these to the exclusion of the other'. 'His work may begin by discovering the outside of an event, but it can never end there; he must always remember that the event was an action, and that his main task is to think himself into this action, to discern the thought of the agent.'

In carrying out such a programme, Collingwood continues, 'the historian is doing something which the [natural] scientist need not and cannot do.' For 'in the case of nature, this distinction between the outside and the inside of an event does not arise.' To be sure, the scientist, too, must seek to make what he studies intelligible. He does this, however, not by 'penetrating from the outside of the event to its inside' but by going 'beyond the event', observing 'its relation to others', thus bringing it 'under a general formula or law of nature', a tactic which at the same time discovers what would normally be called its cause. The direction in which the historian proceeds is entirely different. It is impossible for him, 'without ceasing to be an historian', Collingwood insists, to 'emulate the scientist in searching for the causes or laws of events'. The relation which he seeks to discern is not that between actions and other events, but between certain events and their own thought-sides. In such cases, 'to discover the thought is already to understand it. After the historian has ascertained the facts, there is no further process of inquiring into their causes. When [the historian] knows what happened, he already knows why it happened.'

'But how does the historian discern the thoughts which he is trying to discover?', Collingwood goes on to ask, and replies: 'There is only one way in which it can be done: by re-thinking them in his own mind.' When 'the historian of politics or warfare, presented with an account of certain actions done by Julius Caesar, tries to understand these actions', this requires his 'envisaging for himself the situation in which Caesar stood, and thinking for himself what Caesar thought about the situation and the possible ways of dealing with it'. To the natural scientist, the event to be explained is a mere 'phenomenon', a 'spectacle presented to his intelligent observation'. To an historian, the human actions studied are 'never mere spectacles for contemplation' but always experiences which, in being understood, are lived through again in his imagination. Such re-enactment of past experience, Collingwood adds, is no 'passive surrender to the spell of another's mind; it is a labour of active and therefore critical thinking'. It may indeed require the historian to bring to bear 'all the powers of his own mind, and all his knowledge' of the subject-matter, in this case Roman politics.

From this summary of Collingwood's basic position, there are three things I should like to single out for critical consideration — all well-known difficulties for readers of *The Idea of History*. There is, first, the characterization of the historian's subject-matter by means of the metaphor of 'inside' and 'outside'; second, the attempt to contrast historical and scientific understanding through the apparently paradoxical claim: 'When the historian knows what happened, he already knows why it happened'; and third, the rather puzzling insistence that the thought of the historical agent which constitutes the inside of his action must not only be discovered, but actually re-thought or re-enacted by the historian, and critically re-thought at that. I shall argue that all of these doctrines point to important truths about historical knowledge and inquiry, but that all need some elucidation and qualification.

## III

Let us look first at the inside–outside metaphor. This seems to have bothered some critics of Collingwood to an extraordinary degree. It has been held to fasten upon history a view of thought as taking place in a private world of consciousness, directly accessible only to the agent himself, leading either to skepticism about the possibility of historical understanding at all, or to the ascription of almost magical powers to historians who claim to know what the thoughts of their subjects were. Patrick Gardiner sees Collingwoodian historians as required to postulate 'a peculiar entity' (the agent's thought), 'a peculiar container in which this entity may be "housed"' (the agent's mind), as well as 'a peculiar technique by which the housing may be achieved' (the process of re-enactment).[5] And historians have often been as ready as philosophers to charge Collingwood with mystery-mongering in this connection.

Certainly the metaphor is relentlessly carried through in the passages I have just presented, with Collingwood's talk of outsides as things to be looked, not 'at' but 'through'; of the historian as 'penetrating' the mere event in order to see what is 'inside' it; and of the impossibility of his actually 'perceiving' what he is looking for, as if it were something hidden. Yet in most of what is said about understanding actions in *The Idea of History*, an entirely different terminology is used which ought to put the metaphor in a more acceptable light. Even in the passage quoted, actions are also described as *expressing* thoughts; and historians are assigned the task of interpreting their outsides *as* expressions.[6] Nor is this to be seen simply as the addition of a causal dimension to the original quasi-spatial metaphor. By calling an action's outside an expression of the agent's thought, Collingwood did not mean that it was that thought's observable effect, furnishing the historian with a means of inferring the existence of an unobservable mental cause, which could be called the thought itself. It is true that he occasionally refers to thoughts as what made, caused, or even determined people to act. But he is careful to add that in all such cases, historians use causal language in a special sense, which is quite different from that of 'antecedent sufficient condition'.

Collingwood elaborated no full-scale theory of mind in *The Idea of History*. However, on the one he at least sketched, it seems clear that, far from considering explanatory thoughts as unobservable events, he regarded them as having no existence at all apart from the events which expressed them. In this connection, his views are much closer to those of his successor in the Chair of Metaphysical Philosophy at Oxford, Gilbert Ryle, than has always been supposed. Suggestive in this connection is his vigorous attack on what he called 'the metaphysical theory of mind' — the conception of it as a non-physical substance, rather than as a complex of activities (221). Suggestive also is his denial that an acquaintance theory of knowledge has any application to the grasping of a person's thought — the very theory

12

that so many of his critics accuse him of employing — and his labouring a distinction throughout *The Idea of History* between 'thought proper' and what he called 'immediate experience' or 'flow of consciousness' (294). The latter, on his view, is not thought, but mere psychic occurrence (223, 287).

In fact, so far was Collingwood from holding that explanatory thoughts were hidden, non-physical events, known directly or introspectively to the agent himself, and only inferentially or indirectly to the historian, that he came close at times to denying that, with respect to gaining knowledge of what his own thoughts were, the historical agent had any advantage over the historian at all. A person's knowledge of his own thoughts, Collingwood contended, has to be obtained, as others have to obtain it, by placing interpretations upon his actions; and this requires a kind of historical inquiry after the fact (219). And he didn't hesitate to ascribe to the historian what is often ascribed to the psychoanalyst, namely the capacity to discover in the record of what a man did, various thoughts of which that man was himself quite unaware. It is in this sense that I would interpret his important claim that an historian may discover in past human affairs, not only what has been entirely forgotten, but also what, 'until he discovered it, no one ever knew to have happened at all' (238). Since, for Collingwood, what happened was action, this implies that sometimes, at least, it may be the historian, not the original agent, who first discovers what a certain action was: that is, what thought a certain past event expressed. This seems to me not only a consistent application of Collingwood's doctrine, but also a correct assessment of the historian's powers.

Collingwood did not deny, however, that besides being expressed in his physical movements, an agent's thoughts could be expressed in his flow of consciousness. This is apparent from his description of the relation between memory and autobiography, the latter being taken (rather puristically, perhaps) as an inquiry proceeding by strictly historical methods. The function of memory, he says, is to conjure up a 'vision of past experience'; the function of autobiography is to interpret the data thus provided, supplementing it, of course, with what one can find in old letters and the like (295). Something that Collingwood seems not to have noticed, however, is the way admitting such private expressions of thoughts raises problems for the application of the terms 'inside' and 'outside', as he originally introduced them. For in considering Caesar's crossing of the Rubicon, he seems actually to have *defined* the 'outside' of action in physical terms: it is that in it, he says, which can be described in terms of bodies and their movements. If it was Collingwood's intention — and I think it really was — that the distinction between 'inside' and 'outside' should mark the contrast between 'what is expressed' and 'what expresses it', this

13

definition, although application can certainly be found for it, is in the end inadequate. It becomes worse than inadequate when, later in *The Idea of History*, Collingwood goes on to talk of thinking as itself a form of activity, meaning by thinking in this case, it would seem, a private activity which may have no physical expressions at all (287). On Collingwood's general view of mind, if private reflection is action, it must be thought expressing itself in events, although *ex hypothesi*, in purely psychic ones. Every action must have an outside. But in this case — to mix the metaphors — the 'outside' will be entirely 'inside'.

Collingwood's conceding the possibility of private expressions and private actions thus requires a revision of his metaphor so that 'inside' becomes explicitly 'whatever thought is expressed', and 'outside' becomes 'whatever event expresses it'. The same possibility calls attention to a fact of historical inquiry which his account often seems insufficiently to recognize, and which conceiving the historian's task as the interpretation of expressions should not be allowed to obscure. This is the characteristic incompleteness of the historian's data, made worse by the unavailability in principle of private expressions of agents' thoughts. From a practical standpoint, this could perhaps be regarded as just one of the necessary hazards of historical inquiry. It is a hazard, however, which Collingwood can hardly have had immediately in mind when he claimed, to the later embarrassment of many of his apologists, that historical conclusions can be as certain as demonstrations in mathematics (262).

It may perhaps seem that the kind of incompleteness envisaged here is not very important for a theory of history as *inquiry*. A thought which has no public expressions, it may be urged, makes no difference to the course of history; and the same could be said of private expressions of thoughts which also have public ones. The way this fails to be quite true points to a problem for inside–outside accounts of historical reconstruction that may raise at least an echo of the philosophical worry that was expressed by the quotation from Gardiner. At least occasionally, an historian will surely want to assert, on the basis of later evidence, that an agent reached a decision at an earlier time, although he kept this entirely to himself. This might be asserted, for example, on the strength of a confession made later by a person considered in general to be honest. In such a case, the historian, in arguing from the confession, would certainly be interpreting an expression of the agent's thought: that is, his confession. But he would not be interpreting an expression of the thought which he wishes finally to attribute to the agent: that is, the earlier decision. Not that he would have to infer that any particular private events occurred earlier in the agent's stream of consciousness, and still less that there occurred some particular event that was itself the decision. What he *would* have to infer, however, is that *some* relevant private events occurred – and (here's the rub) he would have to trust the agent's interpretation of these. Collingwood's own way with such an example would probably be short. This is not genuine historical thinking, he would say; it is simply belief based upon testimony (256 ff.). Such a response would be a consistent application of principles maintained by Collingwood throughout *The Idea of History*. But it would surely be too restrictive. It is one thing to deny that historians are, in general, dependent upon testimony, thus correcting a popular misconception of the nature of historical inquiry. It is quite another to deny that they ever have good reason for accepting testimony at all.

Before leaving the question of the sense in which we should understand Collingwood's metaphor, I might mention that his own use of the notion 'inside' and 'outside' in *The Idea of History* is far from strict, or entirely consistent. He sticks neither to the sense which he exemplifies in discussing the Caesar example – the sense critics usually have in mind in referring to Collingwood's view as the 'inside–outside' theory of history – nor to the sense which I have argued to be more helpful for the broader explication of his position. He charged Tacitus, for example, with having offered a merely 'external' view of Roman history, not because he tended to see actions as devoid of thought, but because he depicted his characters as 'exaggeratedly good' and 'exaggeratedly bad', 'mere spectacles of virtue or vice' (39). He contended that nineteenth century positivists reduced history to a mere succession of 'external events', because, in their attempt to stick to what they called 'the facts', they refused to evaluate the actions of historical agents at all (132). He declared that various historians of his own day, using methods he derisively referred to as 'scissors and paste', obtained only an 'external' knowledge of the past in the sense that they believed their authorities instead of interpreting the evidence for themselves (257). Clearly, in none of these cases, does the failure to present what is called an 'inside' view mean that the historian has stressed unduly the agent's bodily movements, and still less his flow of consciousness. It is, in fact, not untypical of Collingwood (and it suggests the caution with which he has to be interpreted) that he should have introduced the inside–outside metaphor at a crucial point, apparently as an important technical term, formulated it in a way which, although a bit misleading, roughly served his immediate purposes, dropped it almost entirely in the elaboration of his theory in other parts of *The Idea of History*, and when he did use it elsewhere, used it in a different sense.

## IV

Let me turn now from Collingwood's metaphor to what one of his commentators has called his boldest and best-known saying about history.[7] What sense can one make of the claim that, unlike the natural scientist, once the historian knows what happened, he already knows why it happened — a claim, incidentally, to which Collingwood presumably attached importance, since he makes it more than once in *The Idea of History*. An interpretation offered by W.H. Walsh some years ago is that what Collingwood was trying to say is that thought — the special concern of the historian — unlike mere event, is *self*-explanatory.[8] This would make historical inquiry different from that of scientists indeed. Yet even if Collingwood's claim is to be understood as referring rather to the whole action, not just to its thought side, it is hard entirely to get rid of the impression that *something* is being said to be self-explanatory.

This has been enough to make many interpreters of Collingwood wary. However, in spite of its prima facie implausibility, the what–why paradox (as we may call it) has not lacked defenders, and among them are critics of reputation like Alan Donagan and Louis Mink. Both concede that Collingwood seems to contradict the merest truism about historical knowledge, namely that at various stages of inquiry, it will be known what various agents have done, without knowing the reasons they had for doing it. A person could surely know, for example, *that* Caesar crossed the Rubicon without yet knowing what he hoped to achieve thereby — difficult as it may now be for an historian of the Roman world to imagine such ignorance. Two arguments against resting in such a commonsense position are nevertheless offered, both of them said to be at least implicit in Collingwood's own conception of action and understanding.

The first is that, in any serious inquiry, an historical fact could not be fully confirmed without at the same time making clear why it came about. As Donagan puts it: 'An historian explains a fact in the very process of establishing it.'[9] This contention seems to me to bear little examination. No doubt an inquiry into whether a certain action was performed would *in fact* often show why an agent performed it. But, as Mink concedes, the precise evidence which would establish the 'whether' would not *necessarily* establish the 'why',[10] and nothing short of the demonstration that it would do so would support the paradox while keeping it interesting. The second argument turns on what it means, on Collingwood's theory, fully to know an historical fact. For Collingwood, of course, historical facts are actions; and actions are a unity of an outside and an inside. One does not know what an action really was, therefore, until its thought-side has been discovered. However, an action's thought-side is precisely what enables us to understand or explain it in the historically proper way. Thus, to know what an action was, both inside and outside, is at the same time to know its explanation — or, as Mink prefers to formulate it:

the full *description* of an action is at the same time its *explanation*. Something like this second argument seems to be widely accepted in the literature on Collingwood's philosophy of history. And those who accept it generally regard it as pointing to a very distinctive feature of historical understanding.

For any critical consideration of this argument, I think some further distinctions need to be introduced into inside-outside accounts. One such is between 'what' and 'why' questions. Another is between what is to be explained and what explains it. Still another is between simply referring to an action and conceiving it as an action of a certain kind. Still another is between thoughts which explain an action and thoughts which make it an action of a kind to be explained. In the present context, I can only *use* some of these distinctions, not amplify and discuss them as such. But let me look again at the argument, bringing them to bear where it seems appropriate to do so.

Defenders of the paradox insist that, on the inside-outside conception of action, we do not know the 'nature' of an action until we know what thought it expressed. They have a tendency to mean by this *all* the thought it expressed, although something less is at times allowed in a given context. Either way, the search for understanding is seen as a rounding out of our knowledge of an action's thought-side. Mink represents this as a succession of responses to the question: 'What was the man really doing?'[11] An historian, for example, who already knew that Caesar crossed the Rubicon, might still ask: 'But what was he *doing*, crossing the river, when it was clearly contrary to Republican law?' In one sense, Mink observes, he already knows what Caesar was doing; but in the sense that matters he does not. He understands the action as a river-crossing; but he doesn't yet understand it as an assault on enemies, and still less as a bid for supreme power in the state. This seems to me a perfectly good way of conceptualizing what such an historian would be doing. It makes a good deal more intelligible the notion that the historian's full explanation, or even his full description, is somehow *self*-explanatory. For if *all* the thought which was expressed in an action has been taken into account, there is clearly nothing more to understand the action *as* — 'thought-wise' at any rate. But this doesn't vindicate Collingwood's paradox. For the latter was explicitly stated in terms, not of knowing what things really were, but of knowing why things happened. The word 'why' drops too quickly out of such apologies for the paradox.

I think that Collingwood himself may be in some confusion on this point. The longer passage in which reference to Caesar's crossing is embedded reads as if, for the moment at least, his concern is only with understanding as finding answers to questions 'why'. Yet when he turns to his example to show us what he means by an explanatory thought-side, what he cites is 'Caesar's defiance of Republican law'.

17

This is hardly an answer to the question why Caesar crossed the Rubicon. It seems more like a logical consequence of what he did than one of his reasons for doing it, although a consequence of which he was certainly aware, and one which could also be said to have been expressed in his action. Caesar *could*, of course, have crossed the Rubicon to defy Republican law; but that is presumably not what Collingwood believed. In fact, he seems to have slipped here from asking why Caesar performed his action to asking what the historical significance of that action was — a question rather closer to Mink's 'What was the man really doing?' I say slipped because the shift is not acknowledged, and the rest of the passage is about knowing why something happened. Such insensitivity to the relativity of understanding to questions asked is a bit surprising in view of Collingwood's emphasis, both in *The Idea of History* and in other philosophical writings, on the primordial role of question-and-answer in inquiry (273). However, since the paradox itself is stated in terms of 'why', it seems fair to insist on the distinction, and to ask whether it can stand as stated.

I submit that sensibly demanding and accepting an answer to a 'why' question requires the recognition of a distinction between what is explained and what explains it. What is explained when an historian claims to show why a certain action was done? Surely never the action conceived as expressing all the thought which, in fact, it expressed; for this would leave no thought distinguishable from it which could explain it. But not the mere event either — the mere outside of the action — although Collingwood himself, perhaps too much under the spell of his studies on the border between history and archaeology, did sometimes say that historical explanation is *of* an outside *by* an inside — as if the historian had to begin by sorting out human beings from robots the way artefacts may have to be sorted out from mere physical objects at a 'dig'. The inside–outside distinction, in fact, corresponds in neither of these ways with the distinction we would ordinarily draw in history, between what is explained and what explains it. As Collingwood himself more typically says, what is to be explained is action. To be conceived as action at all, an event must be conceived as expressing a thought — as does Caesar's crossing the Rubicon, if only the intention of getting to the other side. What explains the action so conceived is a thought which, to be explanatory, must not belong to the conception of the action as it is to be explained — like Caesar's intending to get to Rome, for example. At no level of inquiry is an action explained in terms of thought conceived as belonging essentially to it at that level of inquiry. It is precisely the contrary, however, that the paradox seems to imply.

Still a shorter way with Collingwood's paradox is to point out that, as stated, it really rests on an equivocation. If we are told that, when an historian knows what happened, he already knows why it happened, we naturally assume that the same thing is referred to by the 'what' and the 'it'. In fact, the assertion only makes sense if the 'it' refers to the action as characterized before the explanation begins, and the 'what' refers to the action as re-characterized when (as is always possible) the thought said to explain it is incorporated into a re-description of what was done. If we read Collingwood's example in this way, we get the following statement: 'When the historian knows that Caesar was making for Rome, he already knows why he crossed the Rubicon' — which is true, but scarcely surprising. To maintain the air of paradox, the 'what' and the 'it' have to be taken as standing for the same thing, which would give us instead: 'When the historian knows that Caesar was making for Rome, he already knows why he was making for Rome' — which is, of course, false. It might be noted that, interpreted in the only way it makes sense — the equivocal way — Collingwood's paradox arises equally for explanations of natural events. What happened, an ignorant person might report, was a darkening of the sky. What *really* happened, he may come to discover through exposure to some elementary astronomy, was an eclipse. Evidently, when he knows what happened (the eclipse) he already knows why it happened (the darkening of the sky). Since Collingwood's purpose in stating the what–why paradox was to sum up, and perhaps to dramatize, alleged differences between history and natural science, this is rather an unsatisfactory result from his point of view.

However, the differences between scientific and historical understanding which, in formulating the paradox, Collingwood was really concerned to establish, do not need it for their elucidation. These, it will be remembered, were put metaphorically in terms of the different 'directions' in which scientific and historical studies of an event might proceed. The scientist, according to Collingwood, goes 'beyond' the event to other events related to it by laws. The historian, by contrast, 'penetrates' to the inside of the event itself to discover the thought which it expresses. Put in other language, historical understanding of action is said to be achieved without subsuming it under empirical generalizations or laws.[12] It is also said not to require reference to initial conditions, in the sense in which a natural scientist might be expected to look for them — that is, to other, and generally earlier *events*.

By denying in this way that the historian needs to look beyond the action itself to initial or determining conditions, Collingwood is affirming the sufficiency of agents' reasons for the historical understanding of why actions were performed. Saying what those reasons were requires a description, not of the actual conditions of the agent's situation, but of the way the agent conceived them to be. The belief of Caesar that his enemies were vulnerable, for example, need not be true to be explanatory. In his concern to attack doctrines, such as geographical determinism, which might seem to deny such a claim, Collingwood sometimes says that the 'hard facts' of the situation in which any agent has to act consist entirely of 'thoughts' (316). He also denies that physical events and conditions can, in themselves, be historical causes of actions (214–15).[13] There are elements of overstatement in both of these ways of putting his point. It would have been closer to what he really intended, I think, if he had said that the situation with reference to which an agent has to *decide* to act is constituted by his thoughts; or that actual physical conditions can be causes of actions (by contrast with mere movements) only through agents' thoughts about them. What is overstated, however, does seem to me to be true, and of central importance for the philosophical analysis of historiography.

If Collingwood's real claim is from time to time denied, I think it is generally because it is misunderstood. Karl Popper seems to have misunderstood it, for example, in a contrast he drew between Collingwood's view and his own contention that historical actions are to be explained in terms of an objective 'logic of the situation'.[14] Popper insists that it is in terms of situations as they really were, not as they were perhaps falsely envisaged by the agents, that what happened in history should be explained. However, it is not easy to see how objective facts of a situation could throw light on what agents decided to do in it, if they believed their situations to be otherwise. Nor does Popper's consideration of examples appear to challenge the point Collingwood was making. One example he offers is the following.[15] He found it initially surprising, he says, that Galileo should have rejected a lunar theory of the tides. While puzzling over this, he noted that Galileo rejected advances from Kepler, who held such a theory — failed to answer letters from him, for example. He noted also that Galileo rejected astrology; that astrology, as a theory about the influence of heavenly bodies on earthly events, was well-disposed to a lunar theory; and that Kepler was an astrologer. These, he rightly says, are all objective facts. The logic of Galileo's position, he goes on to observe, called for his rejection of Kepler's advances — presumably to avoid intellectual contamination.

What Popper has described, however, looks suspiciously like what Collingwood would call a reconstruction of agents' thoughts. For one of the things that makes the cited facts explanatory is surely their being what Galileo believed. Should a further study show that astrological lore did not after all favour a lunar theory, the explanation given by Popper would not be undermined so long as Galileo believed that it did. Should it show, however, that Galileo believed otherwise, no 'objective' connection between lore and theory could save the explanation.

# V

Let me turn finally to look at the third doctrine of Collingwood's that I singled out: that in order to understand a past human action, the historian must not only discover the thought expressed in it, but must actually re-think or re-enact the thought in his own mind. This claim has drawn critical fire from various quarters. Patrick Gardiner has seen it as attributing to historians 'a power of self-certifying insight';[16] W.B. Gallie as imposing an 'intuitionist' criterion of truth;[17] D.H. Fischer as admitting into history thoughts which agents merely 'might' have had;[18] Geoffrey Elton as reducing history to 'just what the historian dreams up'.[19] Arnold Toynbee has had the originality to wonder whether re-enacting past experiences, even if possible, may not be bad for the *morals* of historians.[20] It must be confessed that the dissatisfactions of given critics often find support in remarks which Collingwood himself makes. In spite of this, I believe that the re-thinking requirement can be stated in such a way as to dissolve most of these worries.

Many of the problems which Collingwood's doctrine has been thought to raise seem to arise out of trying to interpret it as a straightforwardly methodological recommendation. Collingwood's language does sometimes make it look as if what he is telling us is how to *go about discovering* past facts, whether these be thoughts expressed in past actions, or even (as some have taken him to mean) the occurrence of the events which expressed them. Thus in the passage summarized earlier – and there are many more like it – Collingwood asks: 'But *how* does the historian discern the thoughts which he is trying to discover?', and replies: 'There is only one *way* in which it can be done: by re-thinking them in his own mind' (my italics). Yet it is difficult to make any sense of such a pronouncement if we take it literally as a methodological prescription. How does a person who does not yet know what an agent's thought was go about discovering what it was by re-thinking it? Small wonder that what Collingwood has often been *taken* to be offering is methodological advice that *does* make literal sense, namely: 'Imagine yourself in the agent's position and attribute to him whatever thought you find yourself thinking.'[21] Many seem to have found at least some similarity between such a prescription and such remarks of Collingwood's as that the historian must 'envisage for himself the situation in which Caesar stood, and think for himself what Caesar thought about the situation'. But the former is only a caricature of the latter.

There are, in any case, two very extensive sections of *The Idea of History* that should throw immediate doubt on any methodological interpretation of the demand that the historian re-think the agent's thought. These are the sections specifically devoted to the nature

21

of historical evidence (249–82) and to the idea of re-enactment (282–302), the one comparing historical arguments to crime detection, the other considering difficulties for the notion that historian and agent ever *could* think the very same thought. Collingwood asserts constantly that history is inferential: As he puts it in his *Autobiography*: anyone who answers an historical question must renounce 'guesswork', and be able to show 'that his answer is the answer which the evidence demands'.[22] The 'autonomy' which he is notorious for having ascribed to historians consists not in being independent of evidence, but in being independent of testimony. Collingwood would have been entirely mystified by the charge of a recent critic, Haskell Fain, that in enunciating his doctrine of re-enactment, 'he took the heroic path of attempting to dismiss historical evidence altogether'.[23]

This doesn't in itself dispose of the criticism, of course, since various parts of *The Idea of History* could be in glaring contradiction with each other; and it is true that Collingwood tends to talk about evidence and about re-enactment in different places. It is therefore especially instructive, in considering the cogency of a methodological interpretation, to note the way in which re-enactment is discussed in the section entitled 'History as Re-enactment of Past Experience'. Collingwood's aim here, it has often been assumed, is to show how the alleged method of re-enactment works — and if approached in this way it is positively spooky, with its image of past thoughts hovering immaculately, somehow outside time, waiting patiently to be re-thought by historians (286). In fact, what is said is much more plausibly interpreted as a wrestling with the conceptual, not methodological, question of what it would *mean* to think the very same thought as another person. Collingwood asks, for example, in what sense the thoughts of the two persons would have to be the same — specific or numerical — and what sort of thing a thought would have to be to be re-thinkable at different times, even by the *same* person. In trying to connect the idea of 're-thinking a thought' with that of 'understanding an action', Collingwood's concern is surely of the same kind. In claiming that the only *way* the latter can be achieved is *by* doing the former, he is asserting what he takes to be a logical connection between these two notions (although he doesn't, of course, use this language). His thesis is that, in the sense of the term appropriate to understanding actions in history, understanding the action *is* (among other things) re-thinking the thought expressed in it. The thesis is about the *goal*, not about the procedure, of historical inquiry.

Collingwood's explication of the goal is certainly elusive. If we ask why, in understanding an action, the historian must actually re-think the thought which explains it — why it wouldn't be enough, for example, simply to discover what it was — Collingwood's reply will be that a thought is not 'mere object', not 'ready-made', not a mere 'spectacle' for contemplation. It is an 'activity', which is to be known as such only by engaging in it. Thus we *cannot* discover what a past thought was without, at the same time, re-thinking it. The re-thinking of it, furthermore, will necessarily be critical. Seeing *whether* we can re-think it as our thought will raise for us the question of its cogency. In Collingwood's own phrase: re-thinking the thought of another person is never 'a passive surrender to the spell of another mind'.

Such ways of talking will perhaps seem more natural if it is remembered that the thought which the historian would have to re-think, in trying to understand why an action was done, would take the form of a practical argument. What would make Caesar's action understandable is the thought that, given a situation as he conceived his to be, and goals like the ones he wanted to pursue, faced with a barrier like the Rubicon, the thing to do would be to cross it. In explaining Caesar's action by reference to his thought, it is an argument of this general kind that the historian will see it as expressing. The argument will only render the action understandable, however, if its practical consequences really do follow from the considerations taken into account by the agent. In other words, the argument has to be seen to be valid. And the only way to tell whether it is so, Collingwood will insist, is to try it out; to see whether it can really be 'thought'.

Arguments, of course, have generality. One recurring criticism of Collingwood which this consideration makes it difficult to sustain is that his theory of understanding assigns to historians the impossible task of explaining 'the unique and the particular'. According to E.H. Carr, for example, it was this that led him to deny the relevance of the scientific model of explanation to history.[24] On the contrary, Collingwood explicitly declared that 'the individuality of historical events and personages, if that means their uniqueness', falls outside the historian's concerns. 'It is just the universality of an event or character', he maintains, 'that makes it a proper and possible object of historical study, if by universality we mean something that oversteps the limits of merely local and temporal existence and possesses a significance valid for all men at all times' (303). I take it that the 'universal significance' which is to be recognized in an action, when historically understood, resides in the validity of the practical argument which it expresses. This must surely be what Collingwood had in mind in the following, rather startling passage. He writes: 'If the discovery of Pythagoras concerning the square on the hypotenuse is a thought which we to-day can think for ourselves, a thought that constitutes a permanent addition to mathematical knowledge, the discovery of Augustus that a monarchy could be grafted upon the Republican constitution of Rome by developing the implications of *proconsulare imperium* and *tribunicia potestas*, is equally a thought which the student of Roman history can think for himself, a permanent addition to political ideas' (217-18).

Collingwood's position, then, seems to be that understanding an action by reference to the practical argument it expresses entails that argument's having been appraised and found to be valid. If the historian fails to re-think the argument critically, or if the argument itself breaks down under criticism, then understanding fails. Unfortunately, if this is correct, Collingwood seems to have stated both claims rather misleadingly from time to time. Let me look finally, therefore, at some examples of apparent mis-statement, with a view to clarifying his defensible doctrine further.

Collingwood surely mis-states the claim that re-thinking must be critical when he says, in a part of the original passage which was not quoted above, that the historian, since he re-enacts past thought 'in the context of his own knowledge', therefore 'criticizes it, forms his own judgment of its value, and corrects whatever errors he can find in it'. It may perhaps be suggested that all he means here is that the historian will, in all probability, do this as a matter of course. But more extreme statements of the same claim suggest that he may have intended more. 'Nothing could be a completer error', he declares, with the history of philosophy particularly in mind, 'than to suppose that the historian as such merely ascertains "what so-and-so thought", leaving it to someone else to decide "whether it was true"' (215). Collingwood goes so far as to call the idea of doing one without the other 'self-contradictory' (300). But it would be odd, surely, to say that understanding an action logically required the historian's correction of errors of *reasoning* on the part of the agent. For if he discovered any, this would be equivalent to finding the agent's thought unre-thinkable. It is also quite unnecessary, for understanding, that *other* sorts of errors of the agent be corrected — factual ones, for example. If any were made, what is more likely to need correction is the historian's initial conception of what the agent's argument was.

Collingwood also seems, at times, to misrepresent the sense in which a claim to understand must be based upon finding an expressed argument *valid*. A case in point is the following remark about the importance of understanding Marx's philosophy as an attempt to solve a practical rather than a theoretical problem. What Marx wrote, Collingwood observes, 'would necessarily . . . appear nonsensical except to a person who, I will not say shared his desire to make the world better by means of a philosophy, but at least regarded that desire as a reasonable one'.[25] The qualification which he adds here betrays at least a qualm about saying that the historian actually has to *agree* with the purposes and principles of the agent if he is to understand his actions. But for understanding, it is not even necessary that he regard the holding of them as reasonable.

Collingwood reaches for a slightly different qualification while trying to convey what would be involved in understanding Nelson's famous declaration at Trafalgar: 'In honour I won them, in honour I will die with them' – said in response to urgings that he remove his very visible decorations during battle.[26] The thought which these words, said on this occasion, expressed, he concludes, is: 'that this is not a time to take off my ornaments of honour for the sake of saving my life', and he adds: 'Unless I were capable – perhaps only transiently – of thinking that for myself, Nelson's words would remain meaningless to me.' But this further qualification, if it means that only historians who accept Nelson's professional code can understand him, will not do either. What the historian has to be able to think is that leaving one's decorations on in such a situation is indeed required by that code – and this not 'transiently', since it must be seen (to use Collingwood's own phrase) as a 'significance valid for all time'.

Collingwood sometimes mis-states in still another way the claim that understanding depends on finding the agent's argument valid. This time it is with regard to certain *attitudes* that he at some points seems to be saying historians need to take up. As I have represented Collingwood's position, it might be said to make it a necessary condition of understanding action in a properly historical way that the historian *empathize* with the agent concerned – meaning by this, however, no more than that his appraisal of the agent's practical argument will, at the same time, necessarily involve a consideration of the situation from the agent's own point of view. What Collingwood occasionally falls into saying, however, is that the historian needs to *sympathize* with the agent in the attempt to understand him. He singles out the Romantics for special praise in this regard. The 'intense sympathy' they brought to the study of the Middle Ages, he says, enabled them to recognize 'genuine and valuable achievements' which the men of the Enlightenment missed (87). Doubtless being completely out of sympathy with a way of life *could* prevent an historian from correctly interpreting actions performed in pursuit of it; but too much sympathy could equally pose a problem. Collingwood cannot plausibly make of sympathy either a logically or a psychologically necessary condition of historical understanding.


VI


It is clear that, as I have interpreted it, Collingwood's contention that an historical understanding of past actions requires a re-enactment of past experience, or a re-thinking of past thought, means something rather less than the unvarnished slogan itself might lead a reader to expect. Collingwoodian explanation of actions can include more than what the agent was explicitly aware of thinking at the time; and even what he *was* explicitly aware of thinking need not be re-thought by the historian in precisely the way it was originally thought by the agent, there being as many ways of thinking the same thought as there are ways of expressing it. The only thoughts that will be explanatory, however, are thoughts we have reason to believe the agent did think; and if Collingwood is right to hold that an ascribed thought, to be explanatory, must actually be thought by the historian, he is right to say also that it must be *re*-thought. His holding that the historian must re-enact the agent's *experience* is perhaps more questionable. But when he adopts this alternative formulation, he clearly doesn't mean that the historian must perceive, imagine, feel, move or talk the way the original agent did. What he means is that he must *consider* the agent's situation in the way the agent did.

Why does Collingwood make so much of these slogans? I think it could be said that his whole account of historical understanding in *The Idea of History* is aimed at making clearer in what sense history should be regarded as a 'humanistic' study. There are in fact many reasons for regarding history this way. One of the most commonly urged is scarcely considered by Collingwood at all,[27] namely that, in characterizing past forms of life, historians apply, and perhaps necessarily apply, a set of moral, aesthetic and other human values to what people did — a matter to be discussed at length in the next chapter. Yet Collingwood's own reason for regarding history as 'humanistic' is surely a proper and important one; and it comes to this: that historical understanding, as the study of history has traditionally been conducted at any rate, requires an exercise of practical reason. As Collingwoodians sometimes say, history is 'vicarious practice': it adopts the standpoint of human agency. And this is something which a 'scientific' study of the past, at any rate as Collingwood understands the term, would scarcely do.

## II Charles Beard and the Search for the Past as it Actually Was

### I

If anything has been more discussed, in present-day philosophical writing on history, than the nature of historical understanding, it has surely been the case for historical relativism. A traditional point of departure for the consideration of this problem has been doubt whether historical inquiry, by its very nature, could ever give us knowledge of the past 'as it actually was'. Certainly this is the way historians have often put the problem to themselves. Among the best-known statements of the relativist worry, so conceived, are two articles by the American historian, Charles Beard, 'Written History as an Act of Faith', and 'That Noble Dream', which appeared in the *American Historical Review* in the 1930s, and have since been anthologized and much discussed.[1] In what follows, I propose to restate and subject to a critical analysis the main reasons given by Beard for questioning the assumption that we can ever know the past 'as it actually was'.

Toward the end of 'That Noble Dream', Beard summarizes the case against 'objectivist'[2] historiography in eleven propositions ('ND' 323-4). These are listed in no particular order, and some of them overlap. I think they could be reduced to four main claims, each with some internal complexity. The four claims are as follows, stated largely in Beard's own words.

First, the historian's knowledge of what he studies is necessarily *indirect*. 'The historian is not an observer of the past that lies beyond his own time. He cannot see it *objectively* as the chemist sees his test tubes and compounds. The historian must "see" the actuality of history through the medium of documentation. That is his only recourse.'

Second, his knowledge is necessarily *incomplete*. The documentation itself, 'including monuments and other relics', will cover 'only a part of the events and personalities that make up the actuality of history'. In few cases can the historian even be sure that he has assembled all the relevant documents. 'In most cases he makes a partial selection or a partial reading of the partial record of . . . the actuality with which he is dealing.'

Third, the historian's account of the past is necessarily *structured*. But 'the idea that there was a complete and actual structurization of events in the past to be discovered through a partial examination of the partial documentation is pure hypothesis.' To put it another way, 'any overarching hypothesis or conception employed to give coherence and structure to past events in written history is an interpretation of some kind, something transcendent.'

Fourth, historical accounts are necessarily *value-laden*. For 'the events and personalities of history in their very nature involve ethical and aesthetic considerations. They are not mere events in physics and chemistry inviting neutrality on the part of the "observer".' In any case, the historian does not bring to his inquiry 'a perfect and polished neutral mind in which the past streaming through the medium of documentation is mirrored as it actually was'. He remains always 'a creature of time, place, circumstances, interests, predilections, culture'.

## II

Beard's first point — that the historian studies something that has passed away — is a recurring source of concern about history's claim to achieve genuine knowledge. At the very least, it expresses a certain frustration, a certain metaphysical anxiety, about the task of coming to know what literally does not exist. It is almost as if the very means by which the historian hopes to gain knowledge of his object, the very thing which he proposes to treat as evidence of its former existence and nature, itself constitutes a kind of barrier to the knowledge he seeks. Some theorists have gone even further. They have wondered what reason we could possibly have for believing that 'past actuality', something distinguishable from the historian's thought about it, ever existed at all. That it might not have done so is, in fact, a possibility which it isn't all that easy to make intelligible, if only because there is so little we can say about the present that does not presuppose some knowledge of the past.[3] And any attempt to make it more intelligible by setting limits to it — placing in doubt, say, only a remote past by contrast with a recent one, or only an inferred past by contrast with a remembered one — seems either arbitrary or itself incoherent. Beard, a practising historian driven to philosophize about his discipline by real doubts about how much it can hope to achieve, has no inclination to get involved in what, in his context, would be no more than a metaphysical puzzle. He would doubtless agree with those who would call belief in the reality of the past in general simply a 'presupposition' of historical inquiry, and let it go at that.

Beard's problem is not whether the supposed study of the past has an object at all, but whether the historian can legitimately claim to know that object 'as it actually was'. His conclusion that he cannot, simply because it is past, seems to me quite unacceptable for reasons which I shall go on to consider. But first it is worth noting certain things which Beard himself takes for granted, and which those who use his arguments characteristically take for granted, which, if insisted upon, would put his claims immediately out of court as a basis for denying objective knowledge to historians.

The first is the obvious assumption he makes that his arguments for historical relativism leave intact a contrast between science, which can achieve objective knowledge, and history, which cannot. Thus, in the first quotation above, the historian's isolation from his object is contrasted with the chemist's confrontation by his. Clearly some ideal of knowledge as inspection or direct perception seems to be at work here. But this is an ideal which finds limited application even in some natural sciences. For example, quasi-historical sciences like geology and evolutionary biology, also reach conclusions about what is past and gone on the basis of present evidence. And there is no suggestion that Beard would divide sciences into objective and non-objective ones. Even if he did, the ones that raise problems would not be confined to those concerned to trace back particular developments into the past. Beard would have to classify as non-objective any part of any science that took account of events earlier than living memory — and, in particular, any which, like astronomy, depended upon observations made at earlier dates. Indeed, the use of records of such observations could be said to presuppose the validity of at least some historical knowledge. But if Beard, in view of such considerations, came to doubt the objectivity of scientific as well as historical claims to knowledge, the main thrust of his argument for historical relativism would disappear. For his position — and it is the usual one — is that there is something problematic about historical studies *by contrast with* other, more favoured ones. It is not just that history, as a branch of human knowledge, falls under the general limitations of human knowledge as such.

A second troublesome assumption which Beard himself makes, and which, once again, is often made by historical relativists, is that all that can reasonably be questioned is the larger conclusions of historians, not their assertions of particular facts. Beard distinguishes not only between history as 'actuality' and history as 'record', but also between history as 'knowledge' and history as 'thought' ('WH' 140). By history as thought he means those larger syntheses that emerge out of the historian's reflection upon particular facts. By history as knowledge he means his grasp of the particular facts themselves. This distinction is actually a good deal less easy to draw than Beard seems to imply. What is important, however, is that, if admitted at all as Beard understands it, it would completely destroy the force of his first argument for historical relativism. For the particular facts of history, too, whatever they turn out to be, concern what is over and done with. If we know them at all, we know them on the basis of historical evidence, no matter how indubitable some of them may now seem to be. Thus, if Beard thinks that the true character of the Renaissance or the unconscious motives of Alexander the Great, by contrast, say, with the price of cotton in Alabama in the 1850s — one of his own examples ('WH' 143) — cannot be known objectively, he will need more than his first argument to provide a rationale for such a selective skepticism.

What, in general, is wrong with Beard's first argument, as has been noted by other critics, is its assumption that knowledge is to be obtained only by *inspecting* what is known.[4] This places an entirely unacceptable restriction upon the sense in which we can properly speak of 'knowing' something. If allowed, it would destroy much more than our claim to have knowledge of the past, whether in history or in science. For example, it would destroy also any claim to have knowledge of things located at other places, even in the present — or, for that matter, to have knowledge of things located at the same place insofar as they are partly unobservable, which, in fact, to some degree they always are. Thus the claim to know what is here and now inside a closed box would equally be put in question; and once we had gotten to the point of taking the inspection theory of knowledge seriously, we couldn't meet skepticism about our alleged knowledge simply by opening the box. For inspection of an inside at a later time would not be inspection of it at an earlier time, and hence would not — on the theory — constitute knowledge of it at that earlier time either. All this regardless of what we could cite by way of reasons, or how easily we might normally infer from later to earlier in such cases.

This is not the place to pursue further a general critique of the theory that knowledge requires inspection. Let me, rather, round out my discussion of Beard's first argument with a brief look at two questions which arise naturally out of it, and which may seem to lie a bit closer to the concerns of historians. The first is how much the alleged non-repeatability of past events — a circumstance which might be thought to have a special poignancy for anyone who conceives knowledge as requiring inspection — actually disadvantages historical inquiry. The second is the extent to which contemporary history provides a plausible paradigm for historical knowledge — which, given Beard's worry about a vanished past, it might well be thought to do.

In fact, there is something rather strange, in the present context, about being reminded that historical events are unrepeatable. This contention can indeed be given a sense that highlights an important feature of historical inquiry, namely that when historians investigate events falling under such classificatory terms as 'renaissance' or 'sea-battle', they generally find them interesting at a level of detail which makes it unlikely that their accounts of any one of them, even with the proper names left out, would apply without serious modification to any other. The objects of historical interest, we might want to say — even if this is only a contingent fact — are never exactly alike; and in that sense an earlier event is not repeated by a later one. It is tempting to think that Beard's original contrast between historical and scientific claims to knowledge gains support from this consider-ation. For scientists, surely, study what *is* repeatable — repeatability even being said, sometimes, to be a necessary condition of something's being scientifically known. If a scientist misses an event the first time around, he can always, as it were, inspect it on a 'replay'. Not so the historian, who can neither 'go back' to the original event, nor, since it is unrepeatable, obtain direct knowledge of it after the fact.

But the sense in which events may be said to be repeatable in, say, chemistry is not the same as the sense in which events, for the purposes of Beard's first argument, may be said to be *un*repeatable in history. The chemist simply isn't interested in the peculiarities of individual events. If he is studying the effects of hydrochloric acid on lead, any example of it will do — anything falling under the general description given. For his purposes, a 'repetition' is simply another event like an earlier one in the specified respects. However, in taking an event to *be* like an earlier one in certain respects, the chemist clearly assumes what Beard's first argument puts in question quite as much as any historian ever does; he assumes that he has sufficient knowledge of the past to justify his claim of relevant likeness. It may be true that historians will seldom find present examples of renaissances or sea-battles which are sufficiently like past ones they want to study to make it a good historical technique to transpose conclusions derived from the former back upon the latter; and this may indicate a real difference between much historical and scientific inquiry. But this is not enough to establish the relevance of the unrepeatability-of-history claim to the assessment of Beard's first argument.

What, then, of the connection between that argument and the acceptance of contemporary history as a paradigm? First, it should be noted that anyone who ascribed that status to it because it allowed knowledge by inspection would not be taking Beard's argument in a very strict sense. For even contemporary history goes beyond what the historian himself, like some latter-day Herodotus, observes. It may nevertheless seem to some to approximate to some ideal of historical inquiry, and, if good at all, to be necessarily better than accounts based entirely on relics and monuments. By analogous reasoning, it may seem that, when historians set out to reconstruct a more remote past, the best account would necessarily be one derived from reports of eyewitnesses − that is, from what is believed to have been known originally by inspection. In fact, both of these conclusions are so seriously at odds with historical realities that it is important to say just what is wrong with them.

So far, indeed, is contemporary history from providing a plausible paradigm for historiography generally, that it might, with some excuse, be said to be a necessarily defective form of it. One need not deny that the contemporary historian has certain advantages with regard to the availability of evidence − Beard's first level of 'selection', the fact that only some traces of the past happen to survive, being in this case virtually eliminated. But such advantages are more than offset by the loss of hindsight. How an event fits into an historical process often cannot be 'seen' without knowing its consequences as well as its causes, so that eyewitnesses, by the very fact of being eyewitnesses, are precluded from 'seeing' it for what it was.[5] No one could have 'seen' Napoleon's invasion of Russia, for example, as what we may now want to say it was: the beginning of the end of French empire in Europe, although this might have been 'guessed'. The point is most obvious for those who, being historical indeterminists, would deny that eyewitnesses can rationally predict the future. But even historical determinists generally concede that they seldom actually know the future. By contrast, historians of the more remote past always do know it to some extent, and they represent what they study in its light. Add to this the fact that advances in knowledge often enable historians to give explanations which were quite beyond the powers of contemporaries, and the case against eyewitness history becomes the stronger. More generally, it is a commonplace of historiography that historians discover many things about past ages that those ages did not suspect about themselves. This claim does not, in itself, refute Beard's first argument: the refutation of that derives from general considerations of the theory of knowledge. But it does show the need to reject along with it a view of history to which it may well lend a specious plausibility.

## III

Beard's second argument is more complicated than the first. Even in the passage quoted, two different although associated positions may be discerned, and the first need is to distinguish them. The one, although perhaps no more than suggested above, is that, all history being necessarily selective, the selections made by particular historians introduce a determinate subjective factor — perhaps a value-judgment — into their results. As Beard likes to put it, into every written history there intrudes the specific historian's 'me' ('ND' 324). The other, and more extreme, claim is that a history is rendered non-objective, not by the nature of the particular selections made, but by the fact that any are made at all. Beard pushes this second contention to the point of including as a source of non-objectivity even the 'natural' selection involved in only some traces of some parts of past actuality surviving or happening to be discovered. In this more radical version, the argument is, indeed, less from selection than from the necessary *incompleteness* of the historian's account, however caused. Beard offers as an example of the latter the impossibility of exhaustively describing even a single historical event like the Battle of Leipzig.

Let us look first at the stronger claim. What seems to be bothering Beard is the thought that in presenting anything less than the whole truth about his object of inquiry, the historian cannot help but give a false impression of its nature. Over and over he tells us that the task of the historian, whenever he goes beyond the assertion of particular facts, is to reach a 'synthesis' — a conception of the whole. At times, he seems almost to be saying that his task is to reach a conception of the whole of history, as when he calls upon every historian to declare himself either for a cyclical, linear or chaos interpretation, and when he chides Marx and Spengler, among others, for having gone about the task of synthesis in wrong ways ('WH' 148, 151). More generally, however, his point seems to be that, at any level of inquiry, what the historian has to say, being less than the whole truth, will necessarily be a falsification. The problem is the sense, if any, in which a less-than-complete account of any historical object of study can claim to be 'the truth' about it.

As in the case of Beard's first argument, one wants to reply immediately that, if that is the problem, it surely isn't unique to history. No type of inquiry could pretend to set forth all that could truly be said about its object; and Beard himself, in his remark about the Battle of Leipzig, in effect concedes that this is so even when the object is open to our inspection. Once again, the implicit contrast which Beard wants to maintain between scientific and historical knowledge seems to dissolve into a condition of human knowledge generally. Nor do scientists, any more than historians, even *try* to tell the whole truth about a concrete, inexhaustible reality. Both make their inquiries selective by design, accepting it as part of their problem to sieve out truths which are especially relevant, important, or interesting.

33

All this is worth insisting upon, at least as an initial response to Beard. Yet it seems to be characteristic of historians, and not of, say, physicists or biologists, at least to *say* from time to time that their aim is to tell the whole truth about what they are studying, and this suggests that behind Beard's remarks there may be some genuine and perhaps distinctive problem of historiography. We must ask whether any sense can be given to the notion of 'seeking the whole truth' which would identify such a problem.

What would be meant by a complaint, seriously intended, that a certain historical account had failed to tell the whole truth? When an historian is charged with such a failure, it is never simply a matter of there being something which he could truly have said which he didn't say. It is rather that something has been left unsaid which, according to the critic, he *should* have said — for reasons which could be given. If a history of the French Revolution omitted all reference to the Terror, it might make sense to say that the historian had failed to tell the whole truth about it, and that, in consequence, he had to some degree distorted or falsified what actually happened. But this would surely be because the Terror is believed to have played an important role in the Revolution, not just because it in fact occurred. The same charge of falsification could hardly be sustained by pointing out that the historian had 'failed' to enumerate the members of the Constituent Assembly. Once the notion of 'telling the whole truth' is placed in a real context, it becomes obvious that it doesn't mean telling all the truths that could be told about the subject-matter, still less telling all conceivable truths about it. It means telling those which one has a right to expect in that context. But if that is so, it isn't at all clear why historians must always fail to tell 'the whole truth'.

Certainly there are deep problems about saying what makes some truths important enough to be considered parts of an historian's 'whole truth'. But now, at least, the overall question has changed: we have moved from the more extreme form of Beard's second argument to the more reasonable one — the one in which what is at issue is the criteria of selection historians ought to employ in constructing their accounts. The question is whether specific selections do not import a certain value-orientation, and hence a certain non-objectivity, into the final result: they would seem at least to apply some standard of importance. But let us ask to what extent, and in what ways.

Not all distinctions drawn between what is important and un-important in the course of historical work involve value-judgments on the part of the historian — at any rate, not directly. The judgment that the Terror was important enough to be mentioned in a history of the French Revolution, for example, may well be based entirely on an estimate of the causal role it played in bringing about an eventual conservative reaction.[6] One of the things one legitimately expects from an historian is a running explanation of the series of events and conditions he narrates; and to the extent that causal judgment is a matter of discerning necessary and sufficient conditions, his using such judgment as a criterion of selection would introduce subjectivity only where these relations had to be guessed or intuited. Whether the Terror was really a necessary condition of the subsequent reaction could, at any rate, be disputed by historians without their having to decide whether they approved of it. Thus, if the causal importance of various events and conditions were the only kind that entered into the construction of historical accounts, Beard's relativism, so far as his second argument is concerned, might well be considered a rather innocuous thing.

But judgments of causal importance are not the only kind required for the construction of such accounts.[7] Perhaps there are some special cases where they very nearly are — historical works which, since they aim only to provide explanations of some end-result, may be structured almost entirely by judgments of what was necessary for the result specified. But in cases where the historian undertakes to write a 'history', whether of a movement, a nation, a reign, a civilization, or the whole human past, judgments of causal importance will presuppose judgments of importance of another kind. In writing the history of anything, the question of what aspects or incidents are important *in themselves* is unavoidable; and until it is faced, questions of causal or explanatory importance cannot arise. It is easy to mistake the import of this rather simple point. It has been interpreted, sometimes, as no more than a confused way of saying that the inquiries of historians, like those of scientists, have to be about selected features or aspects of their objects taken as a problem — the problem itself providing a principle of selection for the inquiry, and an objective one so far as the actual conduct of the inquiry is concerned. What goes into a history of England, for example, may be said to depend in part on whether one chooses to write an economic or a political history of it; and surely no skepticism about recovering the past free of the value-judgments of the historian can arise from the mere fact that an historian sets himself one problem rather than another. But it is easy not to be precise enough about what constitutes 'the problem' in such a case. If it is to write a *political* history of England, then selection of political events and conditions, as such, clearly implies no value-judgment on the part of the historian: the selection is governed by the problem. But if the task is to write a *history* of England, the same selections *would* imply a value-judgment — and of a kind which the historical profession has, for some time, been tending to reject, with its emphasis on social, economic and cultural dimensions of the past.

What this sort of analysis suggests is that the writing of a history requires from the historian some conception of what matters in human life generally, and in various departments of it insofar as they made separate objects of study. One way in which theorists of history have sometimes tried to avoid such a conclusion, although one which seems to me hardly to be taken seriously, is to deny that historians should ever set out to write *histories*. They should limit themselves, it is sometimes said, to those kinds of works for which non-evaluative, causal criteria would be sufficient. But there is another, and perhaps more perceptive, even if also, in the end, unsatisfactory, way of trying to avoid the same conclusion which is sometimes proposed – and one which relates the historian's problem of selection back to the first form of Beard's second argument in an interesting way. This is the objection that it doesn't follow from the fact that the historian cannot hope to achieve the goal of presenting 'the whole truth' about his object of study, that he should simply abandon this goal, perhaps settling for 'some important truths' about it. For he might still aim at getting as close as possible to his admittedly unattainable goal, constructing an account which is as 'representative' of the whole truth as he can make it.[8] It might be said, therefore, that 'representativeness' is his fundamental and non-evaluative criterion of selection.

This notion is seductive; it seems to express something that surely ought to be involved in any responsible selection of facts into a history. But there are two difficulties about appealing to it in the present context. The first is that to attribute to the historian an ability to judge the representativeness of an account is to assume that the whole truth which it is supposed to represent is known to him. Since this is one of the very things that Beard puts in question, the notion of representativeness doesn't itself solve the problem of selection which he raises. At most, an account might be judged representative of what was known of the past. But in that case, the question whether it represents the past 'as it actually was' is left undecided.

The other problem is that any attempt to explain further what makes one account more representative than another tends to break down that notion in one of two directions, neither of them entirely comfortable. On the one hand, a quasi-quantitative interpretation might be tried. It has been suggested, for example, that there is some analogy between a representative historical account and a good statistical sample. But if so, it is very difficult to make the analogy precise. And more crudely quantitative interpretations, such as regarding as most representative the account that mentions the *most* facts, clearly won't do. First, it isn't obvious that facts are countable: does the flight to Varennes count as one or many? And even if facts were countable, would any one of them contribute as much to representativeness as another? Imagine a supposedly 'representative' narrative of the reign of Louis XIV which mentioned 'more' facts than any of its competitors, but drew them all from the last three years of his life. Yet to insist that, with a view to being representative, an account should distribute itself evenly over the period treated seems equally wrongheaded. It is therefore tempting to push the notion of representativeness in another direction, accepting it that, for any attempt to get as close to the 'whole truth' as possible, some facts are more important than others. But this would make the idea of representativeness parasitic upon the very notion that it was brought in to avoid.

For reasons such as these, it seems to me that Beard's second argument, in its less radical form, does require the conclusion that selection makes historical accounts relative to the value scheme which is brought to them by the historian. The final implication of this for the question whether history can tell us about the past 'as it actually was' I shall leave until we have considered a further kind of value-involvement that is highlighted by the fourth of Beard's arguments. A hard line can meantime be taken, however, on the more radical form of his second argument, the one from mere incompleteness. Why should less than the known truth, or even less than the whole truth, be thought necessarily to distort or to falsify? To say that selection *per se*, rather than specific selections in specific contexts, necessarily falsifies seems defensible only on the dubious philosophical principle that nothing less than the whole truth, in the sense of the sum of all truths, is really true. Why shouldn't the historian's account of the past be *true as far as it goes*? The fact that only part of a total truth can reasonably be said to be known, still less actually presented in a history, means, of course, that as more is discovered, historians may find that they have to revise their claims about what they knew already. But that, too, is a general condition of human knowledge, not a basis for a special doctrine of historical relativism.

## IV

Beard's third argument, like the second, is less straightforward than it seems. In general, what it brings into question is whether the structure which any historical account necessarily attributes to past actuality can be said really to characterize that actuality. That it does so, Beard seems to say, is 'pure hypothesis'. But this could mean several quite different things. It could mean, first, simply that we can never be *sure* that the past is structured the way the historian's account represents it. Here Beard perhaps implicitly falls back upon the first argument, which reminds us that we can never return to the past to check up, or even the second, which emphasizes the inevitably piecemeal nature of historical knowledge. But he seems also to be saying something stronger. It seems to be his contention that the reality of the past is such as to transcend all structures:[9] that it is a 'seamless web' which any structural account would necessarily falsify. There may also be a third and weaker claim in some of Beard's remarks, namely that past actuality has, at any rate, no single structure: that the various patterns historians claim to discern may overlap, given events entering into a number of them ('ND' 322). These are very different positions, which need independent consideration.

The first thing to note, however, is that, once again, on none of the three interpretations does Beard's argument, as stated, provide a basis for distinguishing between science as objective and history as not. Science, too, proceeds by advancing and testing hypotheses; and in both types of inquiry, the question whether a hypothesis remains a 'mere' hypothesis depends upon the degree of support that can be found for it. Furthermore, as has been pointed out already, some scientific hypotheses which attribute structures are about the past. Secondly, the very same question which Beard raises about the relation between thought and actuality in historical studies could also be raised about the relation between physical theories and the reality of the natural world. If the former relationship poses problems, so, surely, does the latter. Nor is any single scientific theory, any more than any single historical account, thought to explain exhaustively any concrete natural event. Natural events and conditions, too, fall under many structures: the same thing can exemplify at once theories of gravitation, of heredity and of the transmission of disease. Thus, if history's claim to yield objective knowledge is endangered by the historian's commitment, in general, to find structures in the past, this is not a problem unique to historical studies.

Yet Beard's contentions are worth further consideration. We might ask, in particular, why the historian's concern with structures need extend to the structure of the historical past as a whole; how science and history might be thought to differ with regard to the objectivity of their structures; what kinds of structures historians would, in any case, be especially concerned to discover; and how well Beard's distinction between particular fact and structural 'synthesis' stands up in this connection.

Beard almost always, in both of the papers noted, gives the impression that he thinks the historian's search for structures amounts ultimately to a search for an overall pattern of the past, of which smaller-scale structures are but parts.[10] He seems to imply that every historian, in the course of his normal inquiries, stands committed to some view of the structure of history as a whole. This is surely a mistake. An historian can concern himself with delineating the less-than-universal structure we call the Renaissance without committing himself to the view that history as a whole is linear, cyclical or chaotic ('WH' 148, 151). It may be true that, in some general sense, there are just these three basic patterns available to historians. It may also be true that any limited structure discovered by an historian must be conceived as, potentially, part of universal history, whatever the structure of the latter should turn out to be. But an historian can — and I suspect most do — study particular structures while leaving entirely open what the structure of universal history is. Perhaps, since the subject is of great interest, more historians should raise questions about history as a whole. But in no further sense than this could it be said that they are *obliged* to have views about it. This is important for some of Beard's remarks about the degree of certainty with which structures can be attributed to past actuality. One can be far more confident that there was a conservative reaction in Europe after 1815, for example, than that the whole of history has been moving, with only minor interruptions, in a direction, say, of increasing human freedom.

But whether the search for structures in history is holistic or piece-meal in nature, is there anything about the ones which physicists and chemists claim to discover that might encourage the view that they, unlike historical ones, are discovered *in* the object, rather than projected *upon* it by the inquirer? Beard seems, at times, to be saying that scientific explanations, at least, report relations that actually hold between parts or aspects of reality independently of the inquirer ('WH' 149). But in the end he shows himself somewhat ambivalent about the objectivity of scientific explanation, calling for a liberation of history from the 'categories' and 'formulas' of science, as if these, too, were somehow subjective ('WH' 144); and he takes visible pleasure in pointing out that science is itself a part of history as actuality, and thus something to be studied and explained by historians — as if, in consequence, it could have no authority for them ('WH' 144). More usually, however, he takes scientific explanation, and causal explanation generally, to be objective, especially when backed by the test of predictability, so that if historical inquiry could be through-and-through causal, it would presumably attain all the objectivity one could wish. Beard holds that, in fact, in history, strict causal reasoning breaks down. In part this is because of lack of knowledge of all the factors involved, but it is also because history as actuality is not a deterministic system ('WH' 146-7). Even so, he is not prepared to see the historian give up causal explanation altogether ('WH' 149). And insofar as he manages to give it, Beard seems committed to saying that historical accounts may report relations that characterized the past 'as it actually was'.

By contrast with causal explanations, historical narratives, Beard tells us, are just 'selections and arrangements of facts' ('WH' 141).

He gives the impression, furthermore, that he regards the facts as very much at the historians's disposal in this connection. Indeed, he comes close to saying that, since they do not select and arrange themselves, the historian can impose on them any pattern that he pleases. Beard therefore challenges his professional colleagues to follow him in a great 'act of faith': the viewing of history in the large as a movement towards 'collectivist democracy', a view which he derives, he says, partly from a study of long-term trends, but also from a belief in mankind and a conception of what is desirable ('WH' 151). There is more than a suggestion that a similar 'act of faith' is required for pattern-drawing at all levels of historical inquiry.

If there is any plausibility at all in the notion that historians can choose their own patterns, it would seem to be at its greatest at the level of universal history. It is therefore rather unfortunate, from the standpoint of getting a critical grip on what Beard is really telling us here, that he entangles so much of what he has to say with the problem of tracing developments at that ultimate level. The more pressing question is why a claim to discern more limited trends, movements, ages, careers, or states of affairs should be thought not to report the nature of reality. When an historian claims to trace the rise of the working class or the fortunes of a nation at war, what reason could there be for wondering whether the working class was *really* rising or the war *really* developing through the stages indicated? The only relevant way of attacking such claims would surely be to show that the selection of facts cited in their support had been one-sided, suppressing what, if included, would have counted the other way. But this would be to criticize particular structural claims, not to show that such claims are, in general, incapable of representing the past 'as it actually was'. If an historical account is evidentially grounded, why should one doubt that it tells us about 'reality'? If scientists, by submitting hypotheses to empirical tests, discover laws that really obtain, then so, surely, may historians, by analogous procedures, claim to discover rises and falls that really took place.

The way Beard talks about selection and arrangement conjures up an image of what is involved in constructing an historical narrative which, although it has a certain *a priori* appeal, is, in fact, seriously misleading. This is the notion of an investigator's being presented, if not with a 'seamless web', then at any rate with an undifferentiated manifold of facts – like the grid of points in a child's puzzle which can be connected in ways which yield an indefinite number of patterns. In the case of the grid, it makes sense to say that whether one finds a lion or an umbrella in it depends on what one selects; and the sense in which the figures traced could be said really to be 'in' the grid is minimal. It may be tempting to think of an historian's tracing, say, a rise in the power and prestige of the working class in England as depending in a similar way on what he chooses to notice or ignore. But the parallel is a false one. It makes sense to say of the historian that he should have taken into account facts he missed, since they would have counted against his claim to have found a 'rising' pattern. It makes no sense to say this sort of thing of the person doing the puzzle.

One needs to challenge as well the notion that historical facts are like the undifferentiated points on the grid — and in doing so, to question more directly than I have done so far the assumption Beard continually makes that he can draw a clear line between 'particular facts of history' and the 'synthesis' that the historian constructs out of them. What is a particular fact of history? That Bismarck cajoled, brow-beat and deceived the Germans into forming a united nation? That the peace settlement of 1919 acknowledged the principle of nationality? These claims are themselves implicitly structural, as most would agree. They cannot be understood in abstraction from a whole network of relations of the sort Beard surely means by 'structures'. But this is true also of the most 'brutish' fact he mentions: the price of cotton in Alabama in the 1850s. Beard's claim that the historian, insofar as he concerns himself with particular facts, may gain knowledge of the past 'as it actually was' can thus once again be turned against him. Since the facts themselves are known as structured, we seem after all to have some knowledge of the structure of the past.

There is, in fact, a further, and some may think more important reason for questioning the view that the structural syntheses of historians give us knowledge of the past 'as it actually was'. This derives, not from the notion of structures as such, but from the *kind* of structures historical narratives characteristically seek to display. The criteria according to which 'rises and falls' or 'fortunes' are determined, for example, are not themselves supplied by the evidence to which historians appeal: still less are the criteria governing their talk of such things as 'improvements' in education or a decline of 'true religion'. Beard himself, perhaps with such cases in mind, maintained that every historian must bring, not only to selection, but also to the perception of structures, a 'frame of reference' composed of 'things deemed necessary, things deemed possible and things deemed desirable' ('WH' 150). In other words, he must bring with him certain metaphysical and evaluative commitments.

Since it is in his fourth argument that Beard most explicitly confronts the question of the way commitments of an evaluative kind enter into historians' accounts, let me here simply make a brief comment on what he says about metaphysical ones. Beard argues, acceptably enough, that the explanation an historian gives will show him to be either a determinist or an indeterminist. But he also, and with a good deal more heat, notes that he must opt either for naturalism or supernaturalism. In this connection — and rather curiously — he castigates Ranke, the high priest of 'objective' historiography, not only for *allowing* his moral views to show, in writing what he offered as an objective history of the popes, but also for *suppressing* his own metaphysical commitment to supernaturalism ('ND' 318–19). Beard's complaint is that, in that work, Ranke never faced the question whether the papacy was what it claimed to be: an institution divinely ordained. This, he insists, is a question that must arise for anyone who undertakes to say what the papacy 'actually was'. Either the popes were purveyors of divine revelation, or they were not.

The general point Beard is making here is surely correct. A claim to tell the truth about the past must, among other things, be an application of whatever principles about the underlying nature of things are regarded as correct. However, as in other cases we have noted, this doctrine offers no basis in itself for a specifically historical relativism. The contention is one that holds for human knowledge as such, all knowledge-claims having metaphysical presuppositions, even scientific ones. There is nevertheless a nice astringency in the way Beard argues here. It is salutary, surely, to be reminded that historians who offer accounts of the past in terms of metaphysical principles they would themselves disavow, can hardly claim to be telling us about the past 'as it actually was'.


V


What I have called Beard's fourth argument, like the others, has a certain inner complexity to it. On the one hand, we are told that historians, when they come to study the past, bring to their inquiry certain standards of value which they impose upon it in giving their accounts. On the other hand, it is alleged that historical facts themselves, unlike those studied by natural scientists, 'in their very nature involve ethical and aesthetic considerations'. There seems to be some tension, if not indeed a contradiction, between these two claims. In the first, the presence of value-judgments in the historian's eventual reconstruction is regarded as a reason for saying that he does *not* recover the past as it actually was, since he fails to hold up a 'neutral mirror' to it. But in the second, the implication seems rather to be that his account, if it is really to 'mirror' the past, must leave the values in, since the facts themselves are, in some sense, value-constituted. In saying these apparently incompatible things, however, I think Beard is making a single point. And I think the second way of making it, added to the first, will be found to provide a useful hedge against too easy an objectivist rebuttal of what he wants to say.

First, it should be noted, as was already conceded in discussing the argument from selection, that on either way of putting it, Beard's fourth argument, unlike the others, would, if sound, provide a basis for regarding science as objective in a sense in which history is not. It has been maintained, certainly, that scientists, too, must make value-judgments in the course of their inquiries. However, it is not usually claimed that the mere statement of natural facts involves the scientist in such judgments, or that the facts themselves are partly value-constituted, where this means they involve 'moral and aesthetic considerations'. A more usual view is that, in appealing, say, to some ideal of simplicity in deciding between otherwise equally acceptable theories, scientists place a value upon simplicity in theories; or that in conducting their inquiries with a view to the practical application of their findings, scientists may have to take account even of social values — for example, in deciding whether a certain result is probable *enough* to be acted upon or guarded against. We may be reminded, too, that scientists, like knowledge-seekers of all kinds, make value-judgments in regarding certain questions as more worthy of investigation than others. But what Beard has in mind is quite additional to any analogue in historical inquiry of these sorts of value-involvement.

The reason I think Beard's second form is a useful hedge against too easy an objectivist rebuttal is the following. It is all too easy to interpret his first form as making no more than a psychological, sociological, or even historical point about historians. Beard is doubtless correct to observe that every historian knows that his colleagues have been influenced by their 'biases, prejudices, beliefs, affections, general upbringing, and experience, particularly social and economic', 'a sense of propriety, to say nothing of humor' demanding that he make the same assumption about himself ('WH' 141). But I think that Beard wants to say something stronger than this; and if he doesn't he should. For the question must arise whether the ubiquity of value-judgment in historical accounts does not derive from the nature of the inquiry itself — the nature (not just the choice) of the questions asked, and of what they are asked about — quite apart from the willingness, or even the unconscious tendency, of historians to become involved in value issues.

The stronger position has immediately to face the counter-argument that, if historical accounts do, in fact, contain value-judgments, there is at any rate no logical necessity about their doing so; and that when they do, it is easy enough to separate the evaluative from the purely factual parts. It is the factual parts alone, it will be maintained, that may represent the past 'as it actually was'. If describing what the Russians did to the Czechs in 1968 as a 'suppression' rather than a 'liberation' fails to hold up a neutral mirror to what happened, we can still ask the 'objective' question whether Soviet troops at any rate 'entered' Czechoslovakia without the permission of the Czech

43

government. Perhaps no one, not even the most convinced objectivist, really wants historians to write dull, value-free accounts when they come to set forth the results of their research. But it may still be insisted that, so far as recovering the past 'as it actually was' is concerned, the incorporation of value-judgments into those accounts is supererogatory.

It seems to me that the second form of Beard's argument puts all this in a somewhat different light. For surely at some point the question has to be asked: what is history *about*? Even Beard's critics will agree that it is not about natural events, except incidentally. At the very least it is about 'what men have done and suffered': human action and experience. But an historical investigation of a subject-matter so conceived, these critics will say, doesn't *as such* require the making of any value-judgments. And there is this much to be said for that view: that it doesn't follow from the mere fact that what is studied is human action and experience, and is viewed as such, that the historian must make value-judgments. It certainly follows that he must make more than purely physical or physiological judgments, since he will not be considering human action and experience as such unless he attributes purposes and beliefs to agents.[11] But that isn't to say that he will necessarily go on to *evaluate* the latter. To put it another way, if we distinguish between three conceptual levels at which men's actions and experiences might be considered, the purely physiological, the intentional, and the evaluative, there is no necessity of logic that would oblige a person who chose to operate at the second level to go on to the third. If this is the objectivist's present point, it would seem to be correct.

But the subject-matter of history is not adequately characterized as just 'human actions and experience' — this in spite of Beard's own description of it as 'all that has been done, said, felt, and thought by human beings on this planet since humanity began its long career' ('WH' 140). What history is about — and most objectivists would at least begin by agreeing — is the social, political, military, religious, artistic, scientific, and so on, activities of men and women; and the past facts which we expect historians to ascertain are facts which can be recognized to fall into these categories. We have to ask what follows for our present problem from a conception of history as having such a subject-matter. What follows, I think, is very much what Beard had to say in the second form of his present argument.[12]

This is easiest to see, perhaps, in those cases where the historian's aim is to contribute to histories of religion or art. As a number of theorists of the social studies have pointed out, simply to *characterize* human actions and experiences as belonging to such fields may require a value-judgment. An historian of religion, for example, has to be able to recognize actions as falling into classes of activities which are distinctively religious: true piety, let us say, or spiritual decadence. To claim that something is correctly described in such ways is to make a religious judgment — perhaps even a judgment from the standpoint of some particular religion. An historian of art would similarly have to make aesthetic judgments in recognizing certain relics of the past as objects of a relevant kind, objects with at least a claim to be considered in a history of art. The problem, it should be noticed, is not simply that of deciding whether certain acts of piety or certain artistic performances are important or interesting enough to warrant a place in a particular history: that is the problem of 'selection', about which something has already been said. What is now in view is the logically antecedent problem of determining the members of the class of things from which important and interesting cases may be selected. It is as if, to be included in a history of religion or art, a candidate object, person or activity had to be 'nominated' before it could actually be 'elected'. Beard is insisting, and I think rightly, that historians may need to make religious and aesthetic judgments even at the level of nomination.

Perhaps histories of religion and art will seem rather special cases, since they may be considered to be of human activities which are themselves quasi-normatively defined. Even if this were true, their existence would pose a problem for Beard's critics, unless the latter were prepared just to dismiss these branches of history as illegitimate. But the point they illustrate is, in fact, of more general application than one might begin by thinking. It can easily be extended, for example, to histories of science or philosophy, which are also quasi-normatively defined. But it has some application even to political and military history, which, even if less prestigious branches of the subject than was true in the past, are still generally regarded as quite central to it; for the classification of an action as political or military can also raise normative questions. To take a contemporary example: are the killings planned and executed by the PLO or the IRA political acts or are they just organized murder?[13] Are they simple acts of terrorism or are they acts of war? Such questions raise the issue of political legitimacy; and if most political histories seem not to do this, isn't that simply because historians, for the most part, happen to agree about what the legitimate government of most regions was? It is Beard's argument in its second form that brings all this insistently to our attention. The problem isn't just, as his first form may suggest, that the historian in fact brings certain conceptions of political legitimacy, certain political values, to what he studies. It is rather that he may *have* to do so in order to perceive it as having a political character. It isn't a bad way of putting this to say that, in such cases, the values are *constitutive* of the facts the historian is concerned to report. That is, the latter are such that 'in their very nature' they involve 'ethical and aesthetic considerations'.

## VI

Can the historian, working with such a subject-matter, reconstruct the past ' as it actually was'? Even Beard's fourth argument, of course, raises doubts about this only if we reject the objectivity of values — if we are prepared to say that nothing is 'really' good or bad, right or wrong, profound or superficial, legitimate or illegitimate. Since this is a position which I should certainly not be willing to adopt myself, when an historian tells me that the eleventh century was a credulous age, or that the Renaissance popes were worldly, I am quite prepared to consider these as claims about how the past 'actually was', and to accept them as true claims about how it was if the evidence is good enough. One of the things I should expect to learn from historians, in fact, is what the 'quality of life' of past periods of history really was; and this, among other things, would be a matter of learning what their moral, aesthetic and intellectual quality was.[14] However, for those who think that value cannot in the nature of things belong to reality, Beard's fourth argument, and those parts of his second and third which relate to the way particular selections and structurings are value-governed, do have a different force from the others. They show that what the historian tells us about the past will characteristically encapsulate a judgment or recognition of value, so that what he refers to as 'the past as it actually was' will coincide with 'the past as it must appear from the standpoint of a certain scheme of values — political, aesthetic, social, moral, intellectual, and so on'. This, it seems to me, is the most important truth about history that emerges out of Beard's arguments for historical relativism.

# III  J.W.N. Watkins and the Nature of the Historical Individual

## I

The last two chapters have been concerned with large problems of critical philosophy of history: the nature of the understanding that would be appropriate to an inquiry into past human actions, and the extent to which historians can claim to achieve an objective knowledge of their subject-matter. We turn now to still a third classical problem – this time one that has been discussed rather more by philosophers of the social sciences than by philosophers of history narrowly conceived, although for no obvious good reason, historians themselves often having raised it.[1] This is the problem of the relation between what is said about individuals and what is said about social groups of various kinds in the reconstruction of the past. Our focus this time will be on the work of J.W.N. Watkins, a philosopher at the London School of Economics, who, over the last twenty years or so, on the strength of a series of lively and highly polemical articles in the philosophical periodicals,[2] has become recognized as a standard-bearer for a certain position with respect to this problem: a position known as 'methodological individualism'. As before, I shall outline some of the main claims of the chosen author, and then go on to select some particular themes and problems for further analysis and discussion.

Reference to a problem of the relation of individual and group, without further amplification, will convey different things to different people. Some will think immediately of ethical and political questions about the extent to which people are, or should be, subordinated to the social group to which they belong: the extent to which the good of the 'collectivity', as it is sometimes put, makes legitimate demands on us. As is well-known, claims to social obedience on the part of authoritarian and repressive regimes have, at times, been buttressed by the philosophical argument that the individual finds his identity, his 'reality', even his 'true freedom', only through his membership in a larger social whole. The problem of individual and group has also sometimes been conceived as essentially a metaphysical one: the problem of the extent to which social groups possess, in some important sense, a 'life of their own' — a life that goes on 'over the heads' of their members, and which largely determines the nature, the experience, and ultimately the fate of the latter. Watkins is not, in the end, uninterested in these political and metaphysical dimensions of the problem. But the position for which he argues, in the first instance at any rate, is presented as a *methodological* one. It is a theory of what constitutes good explanation in history, and indeed in social inquiry generally. And it is a theory that gives explanatory primacy to individuals.

It is important to be clear about the sense in which Watkins is propounding a theory of explanation. What philosophers and methodologists of history and the social sciences have generally discussed under this head are *formal* theories of what it is to explain something. Collingwood's account of how actions are to be understood in history was such a theory. If the argument put forward in chapter I was correct, it could be re-stated as the claim that a satisfactory explanation of why someone performed a certain action would consist of the attribution to that person of beliefs and intentions which could be considered premises of a valid practical argument enjoining the action to be explained. The so-called positivist account against which Collingwood implicitly argued is even more clearly a formal theory of explanation. In the version made familiar in contemporary philosophy of history by theorists like C.G. Hempel and K.R. Popper, this holds that a satisfactory explanation would consist of a statement of antecedent conditions which, together with certain laws or generalizations, would permit the logical deduction of the occurrence of what was to be explained — a theory that would represent explanatory arguments as having the same logical form as predictive ones, and that would therefore make explanation a matter of showing why things necessarily occurred. Watkins himself often seems to accept the latter sort of theory so far as the *form* of explanation is concerned (although perhaps with some reservations, one of which will be noted in section V). But he adds to the formal requirement a requirement of a *material* sort ('HE' 504), namely that a completely satisfactory explanation of largescale social events and conditions would employ premises which state only the beliefs, attitudes, dispositions, powers, circumstances, and so on, of the human individuals involved. Not that Watkins wishes entirely to rule out explanations of largescale phenomena by reference to other largescale phenomena. Such explanations, he allows, might sometimes be offered *faute de mieux*, but they would not be *ultimately* satisfactory — they would not be what he calls 'rock-bottom' explanations ('HE' 505). Their acceptability would depend precisely on the extent to which they were short-hand for, and could thus be replaced by, more detailed accounts of what happened in terms of what individuals were doing.

With a view to explicating further his material criterion of good historical explanation, Watkins points to an analogous doctrine that was at one time accepted in physical science. This is mechanism, the world-view of Newtonian physics, which explained the macroscopic happenings of the observable physical world as resultants of the behaviour of the microscopic and impenetrable particles of which it was composed ('IT' 730; 'HE' 504). Thus the expansion of a gas when heated was explained in terms of the increased motion of its constituent molecules, in accordance with laws that governed the latter. Watkins is not advocating a return to mechanism in physical science. He does, however, hold that the principle of explaining things in terms of their constituents still holds for social phenomena. This leads him to speak kindly, for example, of classical economics, which endeavours to explain market conditions in terms of the preferences of participating individuals. A similar approach in history might seek to explain, say, the decision of a certain legislature in terms of the reasons why its various members voted as they did.

Examples of the latter sort, however, could be misleading. For, in Watkins's view, one of the things the analogy with physical science helps to make clear is that methodological individualism is by no means committed to giving explanations in terms of what can be said about specific, identifiable individuals. Doubtless explanations in *history*, if not in sociology or anthropology, will often make reference to what key individuals — statesmen, revolutionaries, generals, inventors, and so on — thought and did; and perhaps they will sometimes *have* to do so. But although methodological individualism leaves room for this possibility, and thus even for a 'great man' theory of history, it is not itself such a theory. The information it would accept as explanatory may be, and would normally be, about unnamed, or 'anonymous' individuals ('HE' 505; 'R' 60) — as would be the case (to take one of Watkins's historical examples) if we explained the commercial success of the Huguenot trading community in France in terms of the dispositions of its members, being Calvinists, to reinvest more of their profits in their own businesses than their Catholic rivals customarily did, taking into account also the lack of alternative opportunities open to them (for example, buying land or office) owing to their religious disabilities ('HE' 509; 'AI' 393-4). In most instances, the individualist historian no more needs to treat groups of people one by one than the mechanist physicist needed to make the acquaintance of his atoms and molecules personally.

Nor, according to Watkins, is the methodological individualist committed to the more general, but equally unacceptable doctrine that the individuals, whether named or anonymous, who in fact bring about certain social consequences, bring these about deliberately — a view which, in an extreme form, has sometimes been called 'the conspiracy theory of society' ('HE' 506, 509). What history is about, Watkins concedes, is largely the *unintended* consequences of what people generally did intentionally; thus individualist explanations, as he envisages them, will often have to show how what happened resulted from attempts to bring about something quite different. We are offered, as examples, attempts to improve the economy by balancing the budget under conditions where this in fact led to economic deterioration, and declarations of pacifist principles which, despite their good intentions, actually increased the likelihood of war ('HE' 512; 'R' 59).

Watkins takes pains to dissociate methodological individualism from still another view of the relation of individual to group which, following Popper, he calls 'psychologism' ('HE' 509). This is the notion, as old as Plato's theory of the state, that the characteristics of social groups, since they are to be explicable in terms of the activities, attitudes, and so on, of their individual members, will be just the characteristics of the individuals 'writ large'. In fact, the characteristics of nations, classes and institutions no more need resemble those of their constituent individuals than need the characteristics of gases resemble those of their constituent molecules. Thus, the fact that Christian congregations are declining implies nothing about the shrinkage or otherwise of individual Christians; nor (unfortunately) does the election of good men and women ensure good government. Of course, group characteristics *can* be simply a summation of individual ones. Having noted that a certain nation is unusually literate, for example, one could hardly then consistently express regret that so few of its individual citizens could read.

## II

So much for what methodological individualism is and is not. Are there any reasons for accepting it? At various points in his work Watkins mentions or employs at least the following four linked, but distinguishable, types of argument for it.

The first appeals to a conception of the nature of social existence. What we call social phenomena, Watkins insists again and again, just *are* individuals acting and tending to act; social events, conditions and processes are *constituted* by what people think and do. Take away the attitudes of shopkeepers, local authorities and housewives, he observes, and institutional objects such as ration books 'shrivel into bits of cardboard' ('IT' 729). To put it more solemnly, social phenomena are *ontologically dependent* upon individual actions and attitudes. Should we not, then, explain what is ontologically dependent by reference to what it is dependent upon?

A second argument turns on the notion of what can be an historical cause. According to Watkins, even if we do not put in question the existence of social phenomena, real live men and women are still 'the only moving agents in history' ('HE' 505). It is a 'metaphysical commonplace', he says, that 'social events are brought about by *people*'; social phenomena, in themselves, cannot *do* anything ('R' 58). But if that is so, should we not explain the social by reference to the individual, the causally impotent by reference to the causally efficacious? Would it not be paradoxical to do it the other way around?

Watkins argues, thirdly, that only individuals can really be understood. We may be able to *predict* social consequences from knowledge of antecedent social events and conditions and their various tendencies and dispositions; but we shall never really *understand* what is going on until we reach a level of analysis where we see why the individuals involved did what they did. In order to claim understanding, Watkins contends, we need knowledge, not just of dispositions, but of *intelligible* dispositions.[3] Since we find these only at the individual level, isn't that the level from which our ultimate explanatory premises should come?

Finally, we are told that it is only through discovery of what individuals are doing and thinking that we can *verify and falsify* what we may often, quite properly, want to say about social events and conditions. Large-scale social phenomena cannot be *directly observed*; all that can actually be observed is individuals acting ('HE' 511). Would it not be just empiricist commonsense, then, to say that explanation should terminate in what we can actually experience? And would it not follow, once again, that the explanation of what happens at the social level is to be found ultimately in what relevant individuals do?

If I have understood Watkins correctly — and, since he doesn't present these arguments systematically, I here abstract somewhat from what I actually find him saying — methodological individualism is to be accepted on the grounds that only individuals have independent existence, that only they are causally efficacious, that only they can be fully understood, and that only they can be directly experienced. Let me take each of these arguments in turn to see what can be made of it.

## III

In some way or other, Watkins's ontological argument surely makes a valid and important point. It seems, at any rate, to express a salutary reaction to what may often seem to be holist claims that social forces and structures possess a form of existence that is somehow independent of the individuals who compose them. As Watkins indicates clearly, there is at least one sense in which this is not true. Without the individuals, social phenomena would cease to exist. And the relationship is not reciprocal: social structures and forces could cease to exist without the constituent individuals disappearing, however Hobbesian the fate that might then be in store for them. Individuals are not ontologically dependent upon social groups in the way that the latter are dependent upon them.[4] It is for such reasons that social groups have sometimes been said to be less 'real' than their constituent individuals, or that social phenomena are simply 'constructions' out of or 'resultants' of what individuals do.

The point is one which has sometimes been illustrated by unfortunate analogies. Thus Maurice Mandelbaum, who agrees at least with Watkins's ontological individualism, compares the relation of group and individual, on this view, to the one said to hold between mind and body on the epiphenomenalist theory of mind.[5] The latter theory does often represent the phenomena of consciousness as dependent for their existence on physical events, the mental being said to be a mere epiphenomenon of brain processes, possessing no physical reality of its own. It follows that, if all brains disappeared, all mental processes would disappear too. But that is only because the world happens to be that way: it is a mere *fact* of the ontological order. By contrast, the dependence of social events on individuals is more than just a fact; a necessary connection seems to be involved. A better analogy from the mind-body field might thus be the dispositional theory of mind, according to which beliefs, emotions, intentions, and so on, simply *are* certain ways of behaving or being disposed to behave. On the latter theory, it is logically inconceivable that mind should continue to exist after the dissolution of the body. It is in the same way inconceivable that societies should continue to exist independently of individuals.

But salutary as it may be to remember this from time to time, it leaves most of the problem about how to respond to Watkins's ontological argument still to be determined. For what ontological holists would doubtless want to say is that although social groups may be ontologically dependent upon individuals, *what* they are, once they exist, is still more than the individuals. The familiar slogan for this position — one finds it, for example, in the writings of the sociologist, Emile Durkheim, one of Watkins's avowed targets[6] —

is that 'the whole is more than the sum of its parts'. And in some sense this, too, is surely true. For example, individuals qua individuals cannot have kinship systems, national consumption, political instability, or (as we saw) declining populations; it is only when they form groups of certain kinds that such characteristics (sometimes called 'emergent properties'[7]) come into existence. And when they do, they are attributable to the group. This makes more difficult, to say the least, the transition that Watkins wants to make from an ontological to a methodological individualism. It is one thing to point out that societies just *are* individuals behaving in various ways; it is quite another to insist that what can be said about them (including their emergent properties) can be *explained* by what can be said about their individual members. It may be with this in mind that Watkins himself concedes that the ontological position doesn't actually entail, or strictly require, the methodological one. He nevertheless contends that it 'supports' it, without showing exactly how this is so ('IT' 730).

One thing he clearly must not say is that individuals who constitute a social group are no different from those who do not. For on his own view, what constitutes the group is a difference in the way relevant individuals think, feel and act. Ontological holists want to say that when individuals constitute a group, the group is somehow 'more' than the individuals, even if this 'more' exists by courtesy of the individuals. Watkins will want to say rather that the 'more' is simply the changed behaviour of the individuals: that the group is 'more' than the individuals were before, but not 'more' than they are now. Does this support Watkins's claim about the direction of explanation? Perhaps it does in this sense: that the group and its characteristics will be explicable *as* the change in the behaviour of the individuals. However, it is important to note the sense in which the methodological individualist is now talking about explanation. For explaining groups *as* 'individuals acting' is not explaining why anything occurred. What the ontological argument supports, if anything, is a certain view of the explanation of *what social things really are*. We might call this a 'constitutive' rather than a 'causal' or 'productive' form of explanation. Failure to recognize the difference has often made more obscure than it needed to have been exactly what individualists and holists are arguing about when they appeal to ontological considerations.

It is an important corollary of what has been said about the ontological argument that a certain problem, often thought by holist critics to be addressed by methodological individualists, does not really arise. This is the problem of how the characteristics of social groups can be thought to be deducible from, and hence explicable by, the *non*-social characteristics of the individuals concerned[8] — a problem which, in political philosophy, presents itself as the question how men could ever have emerged out of a state of nature and become members of civil society. It should be clear that the ontological argument, at any rate, provides no reasons for thinking that explanations of this sort could be given — indeed, quite the contrary. It holds only that what is meant by social structures and processes is individuals acting in ways that constitute characteristics of a social kind.

## IV

Watkins's second argument, unlike his first, *is* concerned with explanation in the productive rather than the constitutive sense. According to him, it is only at the individual level that we find true causes. This gives methodological individualism the appearance of offering a single-factor theory of historical causation — perhaps in competition with geographic or economic ones. Such theories are always difficult to assess. For if they imply that conditions of the selected sort are in every case sufficient by themselves for what occurs, they are frankly incredible. And if they mean to assert rather that such conditions, although no more than one type among many that would have to appear in a full explanation, are nevertheless privileged in some way — being, for example, the essential or the deciding conditions — then we need to be shown some criterion of what it is to be a cause by contrast with other relevant, but still not causal, conditions, that would plausibly separate our factors of the privileged sort. What Watkins says about individuals as 'moving agents' suggests that he has some notion of causal conditions as the *active* ones — a notion that would be, not only difficult to justify (with the shade of Hume looking over one's shoulder), but also difficult to apply, except in highly metaphorical senses, to many of the individual phenomena that Watkins seems committed to regarding as causes. For example, he would presumably have to call the collapse of a stock market (since it is a social event) a 'passive' and hence non-causal condition. On the other hand, he would have to treat the failure of a general to send needed reinforcements (since it is individual) as 'active', and hence a possible cause, even if the general simply forgot, or was perhaps fast asleep at the time. It is conceivable that, with further analysis, the activity metaphor could be made to yield a plausible criterion for the selection of causes.[9] But Watkins himself, at any rate, makes no attempt to provide such analysis.

It may be more useful, therefore, to ask why Watkins finds the language of activity and passivity so attractive when he states his position in the causal form. His basic concern shows itself, I think, when he insists: 'No social tendency is somehow imposed on human beings "from above" (or "from below")'; and again, when he denies that either 'superhuman' (or 'subhuman') agencies are at work in history ('HE' 506, 505). Clearly, what he expects from the causal argument is far more than simply a putting of history and the social sciences on the right methodological track. He sees his individualism as undermining any tendency towards accepting social processes as merely 'given', with the consequent encouragement of social quietism, or even of a tendency to regard 'collectivities' with too much respect. Watkins seeks to counter all this with the denial that social processes provide sufficient conditions for what happens in history *independently of human wills*. Perhaps he overstates this position at times, seeming to hold that individual actions are sufficient conditions in themselves, without reference to social processes at all. However, his considered doctrine is simply the following. It is a 'central assumption of the individualist position', he says, 'that no social tendency exists which could not be altered *if* the individuals concerned both wanted to alter it and possessed the appropriate information' ('HE' 506). It is on the authority of some such contention that he rejects especially the idea of long-term economic cycles, thought of as 'self-propelling, uncontrollable and inexplicable in terms of human activity' ('HE' 505). We must ask what sort of reply Watkins's holist critics might make to that line of thought.

It would surely be as follows: that the question whether social processes are ever sufficient conditions of historical events is one to be settled empirically. The way Watkins would, in turn, respond to this is suggested by his coupling the notions of being 'self-propelling' and 'uncontrollable' with that of being 'inexplicable in terms of human activity'. For if he were presented with a case in which social conditions were said to be sufficient in themselves, he would simply point out that such conditions *are* human activities. In other words, he would fall back upon the ontological argument in support of the causal one. This is the way he deals with the charge that methodological individualism denies the obvious fact that people are influenced by the social milieu into which they are born. All that the latter can properly mean, he says, is that people are influenced by what *other* people do and are disposed to do. It therefore remains true that no social tendencies exist that would not be changed *if* the individuals concerned chose to act differently — indeed (given the ontological argument) this would seem to be a necessary truth. What does *not* follow is any exciting conclusions about what any *particular* individual, or even any number of individuals less than *all* those concerned, can do to change the course of history. Indeed, if Watkins were to claim otherwise, he would surely relapse into what he himself rejected as the conspiracy theory of society. The theory of methodological individualism thus offers no firm basis for rejecting the notion of uncontrollable social tendencies *in any ordinary sense* of 'controllable'. When Watkins declares that it is 'we', and not superhuman or subhuman agencies,

55

who control history, it is necessary to ask precisely who he means by 'we'.

A supplementary consideration of a causal sort which individualists, including Watkins, sometimes call upon provides no firmer defence against the social determinism they are so anxious to reject. This begins with the contention – plausible enough in itself – that human beings are not *directly* caused to act by the objective situation in which they find themselves, but rather by the way they conceive their situations.[10] Watkins describes the role of material conditions in history in these terms: they operate, he says, either by changing people (as when alcohol is ingested) or through the ideas which people form about them (as when some natural disaster is perceived and deliberately avoided) ('R' 58). Either way, Watkins insists, it is *people* who determine history, however people may themselves be determined. And he sometimes represents the causal role of social conditions in similar fashion. However, if such considerations are to serve his purpose they must amount to a denial that the causal relation is transitive (by which I mean that it falls under the principle: if A causes B, and B causes C, then A causes C). Watkins seems to admit that, although what people do may be determined by what they think, and what they think may be determined by various material and social conditions, what they do is not determined by those conditions. There are, in fact, philosophers who have argued that the causal relation is not always transitive; and I think examples can be found that give some support to this apparently odd contention.[11] But Watkins offers no reason – and I myself know of none – for thinking that causal sequences from social conditions to what people think, and from the latter to what they do, are *in general* intransitive. The attempt to bolster the causal argument by reference to notions of 'direct' and 'indirect' causation thus also seems to fail.

## V

Watkins's first two arguments are metaphysical: what they allegedly call to our attention is the *nature* of social existence and the *nature* of causal connection in the social and historical fields. The third and fourth arguments are basically epistemological: that is, they are concerned with certain alleged features of *inquiry* into social events and processes. What the third argument holds is that the direction of explanation should be from individual to social rather than the other way around because only the actions, beliefs and attitudes of individuals fall under dispositions which are themselves fully intelligible. To see what is involved in the latter claim, it is necessary to say something both about what Watkins means by a 'disposition' and about what he thinks makes one 'intelligible'. His views on both of these questions are quasi-Collingwoodian, but only quasi.

As was indicated earlier, so far as the *form* of explanation is concerned, Watkins tends to accept a version of the positivist theory of explanation. He would apparently agree that, no matter what material or pragmatic criteria may have to be satisfied as well, a good explanation in any field must at least show the derivability of what is to be explained from premises which include at least one relevant generalization ('IT' 723, n. 1). However, among the kinds of generalizations that he would admit as explanatory are statements about what *individuals* generally do. It has sometimes been assumed that only laws can be explanatory — that is, general statements which assert that in a certain *kind* of situation, a certain *kind* of person or group behaves in a certain *kind* of way. Watkins would maintain that we can explain what an individual does by means of a general statement which asserts only that in a certain kind of situation, the particular individual concerned behaves in a certain kind of way ('IT' 738).[12] That is, we can explain the activities of particular persons (and derivatively, those of particular groups of persons, and thus also particular social structures and processes) by reference to their own idiosyncrasies.

Whatever may be its implications for social science at large, this is an extremely important modification of the classical positivist theory of explanation for historiography, historians being notorious for seeking (as they sometimes say) to immerse themselves in their periods, relating what they find not to general theories of society, but to what was customarily done by people at that time and in that particular milieu. If anything, it seems to me that Watkins does not go far enough in this particularizing direction. He concedes, for example, that although they do not change chaotically, the dispositions of people are not as fixed as those of physical objects. He insists nevertheless that, when an individual's dispositions change, we must assume them to be explicable in terms of some higher order disposition, together with changes in the individual's situation ('IT' 741). That is, although Watkins admits — indeed emphasizes — individual differences, he seems not to admit the possibility that an individual might change his own 'dispositions' by an exercise of what has traditionally been called free will. If that is so, then what is Collingwoodian in his doctrine comes to an end at this point.[13] According to Watkins, it seems, what people do must ultimately be explained in terms of their 'personalities' ('IT' 743). According to Collingwood, by contrast, their actions may be explained, and sometimes can only be explained, by reference simply to what they were trying to accomplish at the time.

But it is a second quasi-Collingwoodian aspect of Watkins's present argument that is perhaps the more important. For although he seems to regard individual dispositions as more fixed than does Collingwood, he evidently regards them as explanatory to the extent to which they make clear the *reasons* people had for acting as they did. What makes the citation of an individual's beliefs, aims, attitudes, and so on, so intellectually satisfying is their enabling us to see his responses to his situation as somehow 'appropriate' ('HE' 514). Watkins carries this emphasis through to the account he gives of certain kinds of social phenomena which, he concedes, elude individualistic analysis: mere statistical regularities which are 'in a sense, inhuman, the outcome of a large number of sheer accidents'; and certain almost automatic responses which people make in groups under stresses of various kinds – for example, fear or sexual excitement – in which (he somewhat speculatively observes) 'some kind of physical connection between people's nervous systems short-circuits their intelligent control' ('HE' 507). But the existence of such cases implies nothing about the kind of explanation that should be sought of 'higher grade' group activities. For the most part, the historian and sociologist can assume they have to do with 'people who behave fairly intelligibly and who influence each other, directly and mediately, in fairly comprehensible ways' ('IT' 732).

Clearly Watkins assigns a certain priority to explanation by agents' reasons in the study of human affairs. As my discussion of Collingwood in chapter I will have suggested, I should myself be prepared to accept his conception of the priorities, at any rate so far as human action itself is concerned. That is, if I were asked whether I think that actions are rendered more understandable by the ascription of reasons to those who performed them, than they are by the citing of conditions from which they could simply have been predicted, my answer would be in the affirmative. I can even feel some temptation to project this difference into nature, wondering with Croce what it must be like to be a blade of grass faced with the problem of the direction in which to grow.[14] That isn't to say, of course, that, like my animistic ancestors, I believe that, in such a case, there really *is* an 'inside' explanation – one that I just haven't yet had the wit to discover (this despite recent popular excitement about the supposed 'secret life of plants'). It is simply that, no matter how much a physical object's behaviour is measured, described and predicted, there seems to be an important sense in which we don't really understand it: we remain on the 'outside'. What Collingwoodians would insist – and the early eighteenth-century Italian philosopher, Vico, was perhaps the first to say this clearly – is that it would be inappropriate to take the same view of social processes, composed as they are of what people think and do. As long as we remain at a level of analysis where we speak only of large-scale conditions and structures, we understand what is happening no better than we understand the blade of grass. As Durkheim put it — although, in his case, with approval — we treat social phenomena as if they were 'things'.[15] Yet in the case of social events and conditions, although we may not be able to understand them in the preferred way *in themselves*, we have at least the alternative of trying to see them as resultants of what we *can* understand in this way. It is perhaps worth remarking that this is a doctrine which has, in fact, governed much of the practice of traditional historiography.

There are various ways in which a social holist might respond to these considerations. For example, he might accept the Collingwoodian conception of understanding, but go on to argue that it is possible to attain this sort of understanding of social processes without reducing them to actions of individuals. There is a kind of *rationale*, it might be claimed, in the way social processes develop and social groups relate to each other: as Morris Ginsberg has put it, society often seems to have a 'mental organization' or 'inner side' that transcends the mentality of its members. Once this line of thinking is taken, group minds obviously lie in wait. Perhaps the most famous example of 'going all the way' in this regard is Hegel's philosophy of history, in which (at any rate, if we take it *au pied de la lettre*) an historical whole, a community, is represented as having had reasons for its direction of development — indeed, for its direction of *self*-development — which can be ascribed to none of its participating individuals. Spengler's view of history (to be examined in chapter V) offers a holistic account of comparable dimensions. Whether Durkheim could be accused of committing the same sort of ontological nuisance is not quite so clear, since, even though he refers, at times, to the 'collective consciousness', he is generally believed not to have meant it. Even workaday historians, however, sometimes take a tentative step or two down the same questionable path. Imagine a case, for example, in which, confronted by an election which left contending parties approximately even, an historian reports that the electorate was 'unable to make up its mind' — this in the face of evidence that an unusually high proportion of eligible citizens had in fact voted, and few of them had changed *their* opinions one iota during the whole election campaign.[16] There would be nothing for the alleged indecision to characterize but the group; and 'indecision' is a mental predicate.

But there are other, and more likely ways in which holists might respond. A second would be to challenge the implicit claim that a Collingwoodian-type analysis alone explicates the idea of understanding. It might be held, for example, that if we can in fact *explain* social processes in terms of social conditions and laws, it would be paradoxical to say that we didn't understand them. This would be to accept the positivist claim that to know the conditions from which something could have been predicted, since it is to know why it necessarily happened, is to have all the understanding anyone could wish. Still a third possibility would be to take the same argument further, contending that subsumption under laws *alone* justifies a claim really to understand. This is the position that would be taken by a positivist like Hempel, even with respect to individual actions. On his view, so-called 'empathetic' understanding is, at most, a heuristic first step towards genuine explanation, and hence towards understanding.[17] To find a reason – an explanatory practical argument – that in fact applies to an action performed is not necessarily to know why the agent performed it, Hempel will insist. For the latter we need to know also that the agent was of a type who would act accordingly; and this, he will argue, is a matter of being able to subsume what he thought and did under laws.

A fourth possibility would be to accept the Watkins–Collingwood account of what understanding involves, and simply to reject understanding as a proper goal for an inquiry that wishes to be 'scientific'. Natural science, it has sometimes been urged, long ago gave up the ambition to understand anything. What scientific knowledge is all about is prediction and control. From social science, too, what we should expect is not understanding, but laws and theories of predictive power – and from the historian the retrospective application of such general knowledge. As will be evident, I am not myself much swayed by the first, third and last of these four alternatives. But the second – the claim that understanding cannot simply be monopolized by Collingwoodians – has enough justice in it to make Watkins's argument from intelligible dispositions something less than conclusive, at any rate as a doctrine about how social inquiry *must* go. One might nevertheless hope that what the methodological individualist is advocating will continue to be done by *someone* – perhaps someone not averse to being called 'the traditional historian'.

## VI

Watkins's fourth argument turns on the claim that only individual human beings are directly observable. As he expresses it himself, there is no 'direct access' to social conditions and processes ('IT' 729). It is concluded from this that, although we may, in the first instance, explain what people do in terms of social structures and conditions, 'in the last analysis' we must explain it in terms of what verifies our talk about such structures and conditions. The terminus of explanation, according to Watkins, must be in what we can actually experience. Or to quote him again: 'a theoretical understanding of an abstract social structure should be derived from more empirical beliefs about concrete individuals' ('IT' 729).

This argument faces difficulties from several directions. First of all, if what is meant is that social phenomena are unobservable in principle, that is surely not entirely true. For example, most of us have observed protest demonstrations, committee proceedings, and (on TV at least) resignations of Attorneys-General; and if it is conceded that we can observe things without observing them all at once, as would certainly be conceded in the case of physical objects like half-hidden houses or dying flowers, we might well extend the list of observables to such social objects as sessions of the Congress and the Battle of the Atlantic. That is, we can often see the woods as well as the trees.

If it is argued against this that the social phenomena mentioned are, at any rate, not *directly* observable, since they involve us in a certain amount of interpretation of what we see and hear, a different problem for methodological individualism arises. What Watkins often seems to be objecting is that social phenomena, being 'constructions' placed upon what occurs, cannot be 'pointed at'.[18] But this consideration is not much use to him unless it justifies the contrast he wishes to draw between the social and the individual, and it is far from clear that some individual phenomena can be pointed at either: for example, the indignation I feel when I find that my car has been stolen, or the speed with which a hockey player gets away a shot at the net. In both the social and the individual cases, pointing will do no good unless the observer knows how to interpret his experience — that is, unless he knows how to apply an appropriate system of concepts. With appropriate conceptual resources I can observe a whole continent and a whole war; without them, I shall be unable to observe even a gesture of farewell. The further point might be made that, for the historian at least, there is no question of pointing to *any* of the things he wants to talk about, whether individual or social; all are alike constructions out of what, in Watkins's sense, he does directly observe, namely the evidence of the past he now finds in archives or in the field.[19] And it seems clear that he doesn't account for past events in terms of present evidence for them; if anything, it is the other way around.

This suggests a more general difficulty for Watkins's present argument. For the principle, 'Explain the unobserved in terms of the observed', can hardly be imposed on social inquiry as if it were one that applied generally in empirically respectable inquiries. Curiously enough, it doesn't really apply even to the paradigm case Watkins drew from mechanistic physics. What was explained in the example of the heated gas is what was observed — its expansion. What explained it is something unobserved — the increased motion of the particles. This example, although it gives no support to Watkins's present argument for methodological individualism, does at least conform to the central claim the individualist wants to make, namely that wholes are to be explained in terms of their constituents. But other examples that, in arguing for his own position, Watkins himself also draws from physical science do not even do that. Thus, as a further illustration of the mechanistic principle at work, he sometimes cites the relation of the solar system to the movements of the planets ('IT' 730). Here too, the observed (if we can speak of observing the movements of the planets) is explained in terms of the unobserved. But in this case there is the further difficulty for Watkins that it is the *constituents* that are explained in terms of what they compose — not what is composed in terms of its constituents. It might be argued, furthermore, that this recalcitrant astronomical example is in fact a more appropriate one for social inquiry than the example of the expanding gas; for in the social case, too, the goal will often be to explain the actions of the constituents — what Watkins regards as alone strictly observable — by constructing an explanatory model for them.

What emerges at this point, I think, is a further mistaken assumption about the general nature of explanation itself, that infects much of the literature of methodological individualism. In considering the ontological argument, I noted a tendency on Watkins's part not to distinguish between explaining *what a thing is* and explaining *why it came to be* — explanation in constitutive and productive senses. Here again, it seems to me, questionable claims made by Watkins are traceable to too monolithic an idea of explanation. For although we do, at times, explain things in terms of their parts or constituents, we often explain things also in terms of the wholes they constitute. That is, explanations can be *synthetic* as well as *analytic*; and a great deal of social and historical explanation is, in fact, synthetic.[20] This consideration alone would make it difficult to draw any general conclusions about the direction of explanation — about what must be explained in terms of what — from the contention that individual phenomena are observable and social phenomena are not, and this quite apart from the question whether that contention is itself well founded.

# VII

I have outlined the doctrine of methodological individualism as Watkins elaborates it, and I have considered four types of argument that Watkins himself advances for accepting it, none of which seems to me fully to accomplish his purposes (although some importance was conceded to the third).

What must now be pointed out is that the terms in which Watkins generally frames his problem are not those in which the relationship of claims about groups and individuals are nowadays most frequently discussed by philosophers of history and the social sciences. There is also a popular linguistic or conceptual version of the problem, which takes methodological individualism to be, at least implicitly, a theory about the nature of the *concepts* used to describe and explain social phenomena. More specifically, individualism is understood as the claim that group concepts are definable in terms of (or analysable without remainder into) individual ones, and are thus, in principle, replaceable by them. Watkins himself has repudiated this conceptual version of the issue. He chides methodologists of social inquiry who, as he puts it, 'concern themselves with the uninteresting question of analysing sociological concepts rather than with the interesting question of ways of explaining what those concepts describe'.[21] He is himself, he says, not interested in such 'verbal exercises'. However, it is not clear that his practice conforms entirely to his principles in this regard. For example, at one point he supports methodological individualism with the observation that 'the Jewish race is cohesive' simply means such things as 'Jews usually marry Jews' ('R' 61); and at another, he represents the statement, 'the English state aims at self-preservation', as just 'a shorthand statement about English people'.[22]

In its conceptual version, the controversy has generally taken the form of a challenge to individualists to show that the linguistic reductions or transformations they seem to be committed to can really be carried out. Thus, in a classical discussion of this problem, Maurice Mandelbaum, having distinguished between what he calls psychological and sociological concepts (P and S concepts, for short) argues that even in the case of a social event as simple as the cashing of a cheque at a bank, it would be impossible by any process of translation to *eliminate* the S concepts (that is, concepts which make implicit reference to social conditions, events, structures, roles) from a description of what went on, without rendering it quite unintelligible.[23]

For example, we might describe a certain incident in the S language in some such way as the following: 'A depositor entered the bank, presented a signed cheque drawn on his account, and was thereupon given the cash by the teller'; and we might try to restate this, using only P concepts, as follows: 'A person entered a building and gave a marked, pink slip of paper to another person standing behind a counter, upon which the latter handed over a number of green slips and some metal objects.' But the latter clearly does not *mean* the same as the former; and it seems plausible to say also that no elaboration of it in the P language alone — that is, no elaboration that did not at some point make it clear that the context was one in which banking was going on — would render the actions of the two people intelligible. In other words, although it may be possible to *describe* what individuals do in the P language, it may not be possible to *explain* it as long as we remain at this conceptual level. How, for example, could an observer confined to the P language come to understand, even in the minimal inverse predictive sense, what followed the presentation of the pink slip? How would he cope with his predictive disappointments when he observes the very same person presenting a pink slip at a party, or perhaps at the bank itself on a day when his account is overdrawn, and getting nothing back? How could he cope with cases where blue slips, pieces of cardboard, or even the soles of old shoes, duly completed and signed, are honoured? Eventually he is going to have to learn how the banking system works. Thus the question is not just whether S concepts are eliminable by translation; it is whether we can understand why people do things in social contexts if we restrict ourselves to purely P descriptions of what they do. What is at issue does thus seem to be what Watkins claims to be talking about, namely what sort of *content* social and historical explanations must have, although what counts as difference of content is now characterized in conceptual terms.

The problem has analogues in other regions of philosophy. For example, it has a certain resemblance to the problem raised by the phenomenalist theory of perceptual knowledge that was discussed to the point of exhaustion in the philosophical journals of a generation ago. The question was whether, assuming that our claims to perceive a physical object are based on raw experience in the form of sights, sounds, feels, etc., any report of what we experience as bulgy red shapes or nauseous smells is ever logically equivalent to a claim to have perceived ripe tomatoes or rotten eggs. It seems to have been generally agreed, in the end, that there was no strict equivalence between what we say in the language of sensation and in the physical object language, so that translation is possible in neither direction. A similar problem could be made of the relation between the language levels at which we offer physiological descriptions of what people do, and characterize it as action, the attribution of beliefs and intentions, in the latter case, taking us beyond anything that can be said in purely physiological terms. In the social case, too, we say more when we use S concepts than we can ever say using P concepts alone. Mandelbaum does, in this connection, make one concession to what seems to him legitimate concerns of methodological individualists (and in doing so, to echo at least faintly Watkins's argument from the non-observability of social processes). He allows that although strict translation from S to P claims may be impossible, a *partial* translation into the P language is required if S claims are to be empirically verified.[24] Even here, perhaps the word 'translation' is too strong: Mandelbaum cannot mean that when we say 'A is cashing a cheque' this strictly entails any *particular* P claim such as 'A is now tendering a pink slip' (for reasons already indicated). However, it seems correct to insist that to consider the S statement true commits one to the belief that some relevant P statements are also true.

Surprisingly enough, despite occasional lapses, it is not at all clear that Watkins would, in fact, reject the contention that social concepts are non-eliminable from adequate explanations in history. Statements about individuals and their dispositions which he offers as examples of what would be found in 'rock-bottom' explanations commonly mention 'voting' or 'investing' or 'marrying', so that whatever may be the sense in which methodological individualists wish to reduce supposed social entities to the behaviour of individuals, this doesn't, at any rate, seem to imply their reduction to behaviour of a sort that could be adequately characterized in abstraction from relevant social frameworks or contexts (a point noted also in considering Watkins's ontological argument). If this is correct, one suspects a certain amount of misunderstanding in contemporary controversy between individualists and holists, and thus also the possibility of a certain degree of rapprochement. For what seems to matter most to Watkins is the *ontological* claim that social phenomena consist only of people acting and being disposed to act; and while he generally omits to specify 'acting *socially*', he seems not averse to accepting this emendation. What matters most to a self-styled holist like Mandelbaum, on the other hand, is the *conceptual* claim that even the explanation of individual actions in history cannot dispense with institutional and other group concepts — this form of holism being quite compatible with an ontological individualism.

## VIII

A further remark might be made, finally, on the question that seems to have bothered Watkins most of all — the question of social determinism. Taken strictly, this would presumably be the doctrine that for every occurrence of every kind of social phenomenon — that is, every kind of thing to which some social description applied — there are antecedent conditions, socially describable, given which it follows necessarily in accordance with social or historical laws. Perhaps that is more than has been held by most people who have been called social determinists — it is certainly more than was held by supposed historical determinists like Spengler or Marx, and more also than was held by Durkheim. It would be social determinism enough for most of us if a claim of this sort were true even with respect to just some of the more important and large-scale socially characterizable events and conditions: for example, Watkins's 'self-propelling' economic cycles.

The point I want to emphasize is that methodological (or, at any rate, conceptual) holism would not lead necessarily to social determinism in either the universal or the more restricted sense. Finding historical application for group concepts such as 'economic cycle' or 'moving frontier' or 'rise of the proletariat', would leave the question of social or historical determinism exactly where it was — a question to be investigated. And although Watkins seems to regard methodological individualism, as he generally states it, as an important challenge to social determinism, this doctrine too, even if acceptable, surely leaves the question of such determinism where it was. For a Watkinsian individualist, the question must still arise whether, when people come together and begin to act and interact in accordance with socially specifiable dispositions, there are social or historical laws which will render predictable certain changes in the socially specifiable ways those individuals will behave. Which is to say, I suppose, that one cannot settle factual questions by conceptual analysis.

# Part Two

# IV  A Controversy over Causes: A.J.P. Taylor and the Origins of the Second World War

## I

Historians notoriously disagree about causes. Argued out, their disagreements should be of great value to philosophers endeavouring to locate historical inquiry on the map of knowledge, the more so since history is a discipline that theorizes so little about itself. It seems reasonable to hope that, when historians reach conclusions about the causes of various events or states of affairs, their conflicting appeals to evidence, or to canons of reasoning, will be made, at any rate for the most part, within a shared conceptual framework; and that this framework — since otherwise their apparent causal disputes might simply be talk at cross-purposes — will include some general notion of what a thing must be like to be an historical cause. It seems reasonable to hope, too, that disagreements between historians as to what were in fact the causes in a particular case will often reveal their common conception of what, in general, a cause is, quite as clearly, and perhaps even more clearly, than their agreements would have done.

It is with this possibility in mind that I am going to look, in this chapter, at some causal judgments made by A.J.P. Taylor in his astringently revisionist and highly controversial book, *The Origins of the Second World War*, and at some of the reactions of his critics.[1] The reaction I shall keep especially in view, although making reference to some others from time to time, is a review-article by Hugh Trevor-Roper, which, under the title 'A.J.P. Taylor, Hitler and the War',[2] has in some quarters become almost as famous — or infamous — as the book. I single this out for special attention because, quite apart from its intrinsic interest, it seems to me to offer, in the manner of its critique, a particularly instructive example of agreement between historians so far as the concept of causation is concerned, together with disagreement about the causal conclusions to be drawn in a particular case. In endeavouring to support this judgment, I shall avoid as far as possible involving myself in the substantive issue of who, or what, really caused the Second World War. This is a problem for historical expertise, and I shall try – perhaps not always with complete success – to keep the amateur historian in me in check. The question I want to raise is philosophical, namely what doctrine of causation must be ascribed to Taylor, and to at least some of his critics, if their conflicting claims are to be brought to bear on each other in relevant ways, and the full force of their arguments is to be appreciated.

It would hardly be feasible in the present compass, however, to attempt to elicit from the chosen sample of historical writing anything as ambitious as a whole theory of historical causation. I shall therefore limit my concern to a single problem that would arise for such a theory: the problem of how genuine causes are to be distinguished from conditions which, although admitted to be necessary (or close to necessary) for what occurred, are seen by historians as providing no more than a matrix or background within which the causes themselves operated. The distinction between causes and mere conditions is one which some philosophers of history, although conceding that historians often draw it, have held not to be very important. It seems to me nevertheless to be at the heart of the dispute between Taylor and his critics, and to be a means, in the end, of expressing deep normative and perhaps even metaphysical differences between them. I shall argue that Taylor and Trevor-Roper, in particular, have a common concept of historical cause, not only in the sense of implicitly accepting and constantly working with the distinction between cause and mere condition, but also in the sense of being fundamentally agreed upon the sorts of considerations which are relevant to drawing it. One can see clearly why they disagree about the causes of the war, I shall maintain, only when one notes their basic agreement on this prior question.

One more word by way of introduction. The cause/condition distinction is one that has received a certain amount of attention in recent philosophy, largely under the influence of H.L.A. Hart's and A.M. Honoré's *Causation in the Law.*[3] These authors observe, at various points, that the concept of cause normally employed by the legal profession is closely analogous to the one characteristically employed by historians. But they leave this claim virtually unsupported in their book, and it has been given only the most casual, and generally unfavourable, consideration in recent philosophical writing on history.[4] I think that the account offered by Hart and Honoré, particularly of the cause/condition distinction, throws a good deal of light on some of the manoeuvres of Taylor and his critics, and I shall draw on it as I find it useful. In fact, it will be a subsidiary aim of my analysis (although I shall say little more about this directly) to test, in a preliminary way at least, the applicability of something like their account to a relevant historical dispute. It might be mentioned also that, at various points in the arguments of the historians, the issues discussed more abstractly in the first three chapters of the present book, namely the significance of agents' reasons for historical understanding, the structural role of value-judgments in the reconstruction of the past, and the relation of what historians say about groups and individuals, will be found to reappear in more concrete guise as part of the problem of causal diagnosis. Given the way philosophical problems in all branches of the subject interpenetrate and interlock, this, of course, is hardly a matter for surprise.

## II

I said I was going to argue that Taylor and many of his critics have a common concept of historical cause by contrast with mere condition. In fact, it is a little more complicated than that. What I'm going to try to show is that at least five different models or paradigms of causal thinking can be discerned at points in their work where the drawing of this distinction becomes an issue. These seem to me different enough to justify their being given separate consideration, although there are important connections between them, some of which I shall indicate from time to time.

The first paradigm shows itself most obviously in what Taylor and others have called the 'traditional' interpretation of the Second World War's origins, and which Taylor himself attacks. This is a view which was prevalent among Germany's enemies during the war itself, which was solemnly confirmed at Nuremberg, and which remained virtually unchallenged until the mid-1960s when Taylor's book appeared. Central to it is the claim that, perhaps more than any other great event in history, the Second World War was caused by the policies and actions of a single man: Adolf Hitler, who deliberately brought it about. As Taylor himself puts it, the traditional view holds that the cause of the war is to be sought *in Hitler's will alone* ('T' 34, 168). This is certainly to state it strongly, but the historical literature Taylor has in mind does at least approach this dictum as a limit. Thus Trevor-Roper, in support of the contention that Hitler was, at any rate, the chief cause of the war, attributes to him an aggressive policy aimed at European domination which was 'deliberately planned'. And Walter Hofer, in a book called *War Premeditated*, after comparing the role of Hitler in the thirties with that of the Kaiser two decades earlier, finds himself driven to the conclusion that, whereas the First World War 'broke out', the Second was deliberately 'unleashed'.[5] Others have spoken in similar terms.

The logic of this traditional position seems to be the following: that Hitler must be regarded as the cause of the war because, unlike any of the other statesmen involved, he fully intended that war should result from what he did, the actions of the others therefore being relegated to the status of mere conditions. The general principle implicit here — that people cause those consequences of their actions they fully intend — seems acceptable as far as it goes. It formulates a perfectly familiar paradigm of causal connection: one which, as Hart and Honoré have remarked, is entrenched, not only in common sense, but also in the law, as the rule that, for purposes of causal attribution, 'intended consequences can never be too remote'.[6] Taylor seems occasionally to misunderstand the nature of such attribution: for example, when he caricatures his opponents' position as implying that the German Führer somehow managed to do 'everything himself, even driving the trains and filling the gas chambers'. Hitler was only 'fuel to an existing engine', he reminds us; he would have 'counted for nothing without the support and cooperation of the German people' ('T' 26). But true as this may be, it doesn't, in itself, invalidate the claim that it was Hitler who caused the war. For holding that a person causes what he intends need not commit us to the absurd idea that a causally significant intention must itself be a sufficient condition of what it causes. It is quite enough that it be a necessary one. Of course, it must *be* a necessary one.[7] The traditional claim would indeed be undermined if it could be shown that Hitler or his intentions made no difference to what occurred. Taylor occasionally flirts with such possibilities. But denying the indispensability of Hitler's own contributions to the coming of the war is not his usual stance.

What he does rather — quite often at any rate — is accept the logic of the paradigm and argue that Hitler did not cause the war because he did not intend it. He was more an opportunist than a schemer, Taylor maintains. Like most practical statesmen, he seldom made distant plans. Of course, he did have some general aims, notably the destruction of the international system created by the Treaty of Versailles, and the restoration of Germany to a dominant position in Europe once again. He was quite willing to exploit situations to those ends as opportunities arose, and even to threaten war from time to time; but that is far from saying that he actually intended to fight one. The war that came was something that, like some other statesmen of the time, Hitler blundered into. He simply lost control, and found himself involved finally in a war that he neither intended nor wanted ('T' 10, 100, 314). Or so, at least, says Taylor when most directly challenging the attribution of a causal role to Hitler in accordance with the first paradigm.[8]

A critic like Trevor-Roper takes a very different view. He sees Hitler as having had far more ambitious aims, and as having been far less casual about their implementation.[9] At very least, he argues, Hitler meant to seize, by whatever means proved necessary, massive territories in the East some time before 1945 — territories which would provide Germany with 'living-space' for a future population of more than 200 millions, and make possible her rise to the rank of a super-power. He also had definite, if still flexible, ideas about how this was to be accomplished. For example, he recognized the necessity of neutralizing the Western Powers before advancing on Russia — by force if diplomacy proved ineffective. And long before 1939 he had prescribed for a country like Poland only a choice between joining Germany in an offensive alliance against the Soviets, or being invaded. Certainly he hoped to be able to take many of the initial steps toward his ultimate goals without war — for example, the annexation of Austria and Czechoslovakia, which he saw, not as an end in itself, but as providing a necessary base for eastern expansion. But he never deluded himself into thinking that war would not be necessary in the end. In making such a response to Taylor, Trevor-Roper commits himself as much as Taylor did to the logic of the first paradigm: his objections would lose their point if he did not. In both cases, the causal significance assigned to Hitler is grounded in prior judgments about what his intentions really were.

One reason why Taylor and critics like Trevor-Roper differ about Hitler's aims and intentions is that they differ about what counts as evidence for them. Taylor's revisionist picture of a non-warlike Hitler, unlike the more usual case of historical revisionism, is largely based, not on citation of new evidence, but on re-interpretations of what was already known. And Taylor's re-interpretations have often been attacked as quite irresponsibly *ad hoc*. He has been said to select only what supports his own view, or to twist the meaning of such evidence as does not.[10] A famous alleged instance of the latter is his treatment of the so-called Hossbach Memorandum of November 1937, which is regarded by Trevor-Roper and others as highly revelatory of Hitler's aggressive intentions — it does, after all, envisage annexations of neighbouring countries, and it expresses doubt that Germany's goals could be achieved without war ('TR' 92-93). Taylor brushes this document aside (Trevor-Roper says 'puffs' it aside) as mere talk for purposes that had nothing to do with Hitler's foreign policy ('T' 20-2, 170-1). Similarly rejected either as daydreaming, or as talking for effect, or as rationalization after the fact, are many warlike pronouncements found in documents ranging from *Mein Kampf* to the record of Hitler's talks with his generals deep in occupied Russia in 1941 — all this on the principle, sound enough in itself, that the historian

73

must keep in mind not only what a document says, but also why it came into existence. Taylor has been accused of freely imagining why documents come into existence — indeed, of having invented in the process a whole new historical genre: 'imaginable history'.[11]

Obviously it is a question of some importance for the theory of historiography how such different conclusions could be drawn by competent historians from basically the same body of evidence. What matters for present purposes, however, is less the relative soundness of the various evidential arguments offered than the extent to which the first causal paradigm can be seen to be at work in them even when they disagree. If, in fact, its operation is, at times, rather less apparent than what I have said already might lead one to expect, this is due partly, I think, to three sources of possible confusion, all of some philosophical interest, that greatly complicate the dispute between Taylor and his critics, and which a thorough analysis of the controversy would have to take more systematically into account than is possible here.

The first is an unfortunate lack of precision in the question, 'Did Hitler really intend the Second World War?', as Taylor conjures with it. What exactly would Hitler have had to intend, we need to know, before it would be admitted that he intended 'the Second World War'? Must he have aimed at an outbreak specifically in 1939? This interpretation is encouraged by the emphasis Taylor often places on the date when attacking his 'traditionalist' opponents, as if a war that broke out earlier than Hitler would have preferred could not be said to have been a war intended by him (Taylor notes Hitler's designation of the period 1943–5 as the optimum one for German military adventure, although he doesn't take this to indicate anything precise ('T' 169, 267)). Must he have intended military operations against Britain and France as well as against Poland? Apparently so, since Taylor thinks it a problem for his opponents that Hitler hoped almost to the last moment to avoid hostilities with the West and Poland simultaneously ('T' 336). Must the war have been envisaged antecedently as a struggle of considerable duration and ultimately global scope? Again, apparently so, given the importance Taylor assigns to the fact that, right up to the invasion of Russia, the German army was essentially a front-line force, with little in the way of reserves, as if an intention to launch a series of blitzkriegs wouldn't count ('T' 17, 267). And how long in advance would Hitler have had to form the relevant intention, whatever its actual content, for Taylor to have to concede his own thesis refuted? He allows at one point, even if only in a roundabout way, that Hitler was committed to war by midsummer 1939 ('T' 266). But if this was too late to show Taylor's thesis wrong, how much earlier must Hitler have committed himself?

In fact, Taylor tends to move from one to another of such possible specifications of what Hitler is supposed to have intended, as the tactic of the moment requires. If he has to concede that Hitler intended war in the East, he denies that he intended it also in the West ('T' 99, 136); if he has to allow that he intended it with Britain and France, he denies that he intended it to be serious ('T' 20); if he has to allow that he intended it sooner or later, he denies that he intended it in 1939, and so on ('T' 136–7). The obvious danger of such a shifting mode of defence is that, in the end, all that he will be maintaining is that Hitler did not, from the very beginning, intend the Second World War *exactly as it happened*, in all its detail. If, in fact, he stops somewhat short of that final degeneration of his claim, he seems often, at any rate, to concern himself with attributions of intention that few opponents would feel themselves committed to when insisting that Hitler intended the Second World War. In fairness to Taylor, it might be remarked that no one precise understanding of the expression, 'intending the Second World War', will be found in the writings of those historians against whom he is reacting. It might be noted, too, that he himself takes an important step towards clarifying the question at issue, and thus towards making the controversy more significant, when, in a rare reply to his critics, he announces that by 'Second World War' he meant only 'the minor European conflict that broke out in 1939', not the world conflagration that had its true beginning with the German invasion of Russia in 1941.[12] This makes irrelevant at least some of the more extreme formulations of Hitler's possible intentions that Taylor nevertheless takes the trouble to attack: for example, that he intended to fight a war to make him 'master of the world'; or even that (like some 'second Attila') he sought war 'for its own sake' ('T' 10, 98). However, it still often leaves it extraordinarily obscure exactly what is being debated when the question is asked whether Hitler really intended 'the war'.

A second source of possible confusion that makes it difficult at times to see clearly the workings of the first causal paradigm concerns differences between Taylor and his critics, not about what Hitler is supposed to have intended, but about what it means to say that he intended it. As a number of his reviewers have noted, Taylor often talks as if a person cannot seriously be said to intend a certain result unless he has a clear conception of the means to be employed to attain it. To intend, he often insists, implies having a *plan*[13] – this to be understood as 'something which is prepared and worked out in detail' ('T' 24). According to Taylor, Hitler had nothing that could, in this sense, be called a plan for a European war. Indeed, there is nothing that could properly be called a plan, he claims, even in that series of individual crises which are generally agreed to have constituted the main steps leading to the final outbreak – the Rhineland, Austria, the Sudetenland, Prague, Memel, Danzig.[14] In support of this contention, Taylor notes such events as the massive breakdown of German transport during the unopposed invasion of Austria, and the fact that, even during the Russian campaign, a surprising amount had to be improvised ('T' 188, 269). Some of Taylor's opponents have given him the lie direct on this point: Trevor-Roper, for example, doesn't hesitate to ascribe a definite 'programme' of aggression to Hitler[15] — even a 'blueprint' ('TR' 90) (Taylor himself remarking that Hitler 'produced a blueprint nearly every time he made a speech' ('T' 22)). Only slightly more moderate is the position of P.A. Reynolds: that to point out that the events of the thirties failed to develop 'precisely according to Hitler's plans and intentions' is quite irrelevant to the essential argument, namely that 'the succession of crises represented stages in a broad plan the aims of which could not be achieved without war, and that Hitler recognized this.'[16]

Reynolds goes so far as to characterize Taylor's assimilation of intending to detailed planning as a piece of 'verbal quibbling'. In fact, Taylor's point is not just a quibble. For there is indeed some sort of conceptual connection, if not a strictly necessary one, between intending a certain result and having some conception of the means by which it may be obtained. It seems logically odd, at any rate, to speak of a person's intending something, by contrast with merely wanting it or hoping for it, and not having the slightest idea of how to go about getting it. We should be hard put in such a case to give a sense to the claim that a person had a genuine intention. But even as Taylor represents Hitler, and certainly as the 'traditionalists' do, this seems not to have been his sort of case. What is generally claimed, even by Trevor-Roper, is only that Hitler was *flexible*[17] as to means ·(he would accomplish his aims, as he said, '*so oder so*' ('TR' 90)). And some such flexibility is quite compatible with having fixed goals. Thus the question is not whether Hitler had precise plans, but whether he had a sufficiently clear idea of possible means for it to be intelligible to say that he intended the war (supposing we have cleared up exactly what is meant by 'the war'). It is somewhat surprising to find that, after apparently rejecting this conceptual position in theory, Taylor in effect concedes it in practice. For although he refuses to ascribe to Hitler an intention to bring about the war, he makes no difficulty at all about ascribing to him many other important intentions: for example, those of undoing the 'slave' Treaty of Versailles, and of making Germany once again 'the dominant power in Europe' ('T' 14-15, 97, 171). And he does this without even trying to show that these intentions were accompanied by precise plans — indeed, at many points he says flatly that they were not.

However, neither the problem of what is to be meant by 'the war', nor that of the logical relation between intending and planning, need be seen as throwing serious doubt upon the claim that the first causal paradigm actually functions in the dispute. What is indicated is chiefly a need for clarification. By contrast, still a third source of possible confusion, and one that raises still a further difficulty of a conceptual sort, does begin, I think, to suggest at least a limit to the range of application of the first paradigm — a limit that makes it unlikely that it will provide a rationale for the whole causal controversy we have in view. This third problem is whether, in order to claim that Hitler caused the war because he intended it, it is necessary to show that he intended it *as such*. Even a 'traditionalist' like Trevor-Roper some-times hesitates to go that far. The most that would generally be claimed is that Hitler well knew that what he was doing would probably lead to war, ar.d that he accepted this *as its necessary consequence*. The question is whether this is enough to bring the case under the principle that people cause what they intend.

G.F. Hudson puts in the following way what I think might be a commonly accepted answer. He concedes — perhaps too easily — that even in the case of the Polish crisis, Hitler would have preferred to gain his objectives without war (according to Taylor himself, what Hitler really wanted was 'the fruits of total victory without total war' ('T' 16)). He nevertheless maintains that, although Hitler hoped that various manoeuvres, such as the signing of the Nazi–Soviet Pact before the march on Poland, 'might deter Britain and France from intervening', and thus avoid a general war, he showed that 'he did not count on it and was determined to go through with his attack even if they did intervene.' In other words, he says, Hitler 'conditionally willed a European war, of which he had formal and solemn warning'.[18] P.A. Reynolds makes a similar point. 'In law and in common sense,' he observes, 'the consequence of an action is presumed to have been intended if a reasonable man would suppose that the particular con-sequence would follow from the action in question.' And he goes on: 'Whether Hitler was a reasonable man or not', his actions were 'such that any sane man would expect eventually to lead to war, protest as Taylor may (and Hitler sometimes did) that this was not his intention.'[19] Actually, what is relevant, one would think, is not what any reasonable man, or even any sane man, would have expected; it is what Hitler in fact expected. But by the latter test, too, it seems appropriate to say that, on the account generally offered by both Taylor and his critics, Hitler *conditionally willed* the war.

Now the idea of conditional willing is doubtless a problematic as well as an intriguing one, which it would be of independent phil-osophical interest to try to refine and develop.[20] It will be enough for present purposes, however, if I simply point out certain conse-quences, both for Taylor and for his critics, of accepting or rejecting this idea when making causal judgments in accordance with the first paradigm. The problem for Taylor's critics is that, if they argue that

Hitler caused the war because he intended it, but only in the extended, 'conditional' sense of 'intend', it is highly unlikely that they will be able to avoid the (to them) quite unwelcome conclusion that Hitler's enemies did so too (there being nothing in the first paradigm to exclude the possibility that several antecedent necessary conditions may satisfy the requirements for causal status). For if the adoption of a policy that accepts war as a likely consequence makes it possible to attribute causal status to Hitler, why should not the refusal of the Poles to accede to German demands, or the offering of the guarantee by the British, also be regarded as causes? It doesn't help to point out that Hitler's enemies hoped that war would not be a consequence of their policies, even in 1939, since, as we have seen, the same may be said of Hitler, even by the 'traditionalists'. The difficulty is all the greater if the notion of conditional willing is extended to include cases where a certain result is merely *risked*, as Hitler is sometimes said merely to have risked the outbreak of a major war.[21]

On the other hand, if Taylor himself, in order to maintain his own thesis, argues that Hitler didn't cause the war because he didn't fully intend it — conditional willing being ruled out of consideration — he too will fall into a certain difficulty. For his own position, at least in his more forthright moments, is not just that Hitler didn't cause the war: it is that certain other people did: for example, Chamberlain, Daladier and Beck. And he cannot make a plausible case for this further, positive, conclusion as long as he argues on the first causal paradigm. For one extravagance of which Taylor is never guilty is holding that Hitler's enemies intended the war *un*conditionally — or, at any rate, in any logically stronger sense than Hitler did himself. Both apparently accepted the risk; neither wanted war if they could gain their ends otherwise; formally speaking, they would seem to have been in the same position. Thus, if Taylor is to make good his positive thesis about the war's causes as well as his negative one — his view of Hitler's enemies as well as of Hitler himself — some other model of causal thinking than the first paradigm will be required: some model that will give purchase to the distinction between causes and mere background conditions, given a number of actions of a number of agents *none* of whom is regarded as having unconditionally intended the result. The same problem arises for the negative thesis of the 'traditionalists', given a situation in which it is allowed that many, and perhaps most, of the agents concerned conditionally intended what occurred.

## III

I have tried to show that, even though it may get them into trouble at certain points, both Taylor and his critics frequently argue in ways that assume the acceptability of the first causal paradigm. However, they do not always argue in these ways. This is particularly evident in the critique of Taylor by Trevor-Roper, which often ascribes to him very different, and rather more subtle, sorts of reasons for asserting that Hitler caused the war than that he intended it, and performed actions which were necessary to its coming about. I now want to argue that, in the responses of a number of Taylor's opponents, including Trevor-Roper, as well as in much of what Taylor himself has to say, two further paradigms of causal thinking can be seen to be at work. One of these — I'll refer to it as *paradigm two* — is signalized by Taylor's insistence that Hitler's aims and methods were, after all, only those to be expected of a German leader in his position: they were 'normal'. The other — I'll call it *paradigm three* — is associated with Taylor's account of Hitler as much less an initiator of the events and circumstances of his time than is generally supposed by the 'traditionalists'. As will appear, I think there are important similarities between the problems posed and the strategies of argument employed by these two further paradigms; but they turn on distinguishable ideas, and I shall consider them in turn. I might mention that my account of examples apparently falling under them corresponds in essentials to the thesis of Hart and Honoré that, among the more important ideas involved in the identification of fully causal conditions, are those of 'abnormality' and 'voluntariness'.[22]

## IV

Taylor never tires of the theme that, for all his bluster, his arrogance and cruelty, his reactionary social ideals, and his unspeakable racial views, in the area of foreign policy Hitler was just an ordinary German statesman pursuing goals which German diplomacy had always pursued ('T' 97, 14). These goals he sees, indeed, as the sort that the leader of any great power would naturally have pursued, given similar resources, history, and territorial position. Hitler was doubtless guilty of 'many wicked acts', Taylor concedes; but his actual policy in foreign affairs, he holds, was no more wicked than that of immediate predecessors like Stresemann and Brüning, who have generally been applauded for their efforts to rehabilitate their country. Even in his conduct of foreign policy, Taylor maintains, Hitler was not fundamentally different from the leaders of other European powers. The positions of all of them were based ultimately on force, and all defended their interests from time to time by threatening force ('T' 100). In fact, the Treaty of Versailles had placed Germany in a highly 'artificial' position.[23] She was left intact, potentially still the most powerful

79

nation in Europe, but denied her 'natural weight'. The post-war settlement, as Taylor sees it, was a most unnatural compromise between accepting the realities of the Great Power world antecedently existing and opting for a quite different one by breaking Germany up. Given all this, there was nothing really strange about either Hitler's aims or his methods of pursuing them. What was strange, and is far more justifiably regarded as the cause of the war, was the failure of the Western Powers to adopt a 'realistic' attitude to German aspirations: one that abandoned the foolish hope of holding her down indefinitely. A particularly poignant example of this lack of 'realism' was the guarantee to Poland, which committed Great Britain to a blind, ineffective, and ultimately disastrous defence of the *status quo*.

Trevor-Roper will have none of this picture of Hitler as a normal German statesman. His aims, he says, far exceeded those of Stresemann and Brüning, or of any of the traditional German nationalists, who would have been quite satisfied with the frontiers of 1914. Hitler himself expressed contempt for such limited ambitions, and made it clear that he would regard as ultimately unsatisfactory even a restoration of the enormous gains made in 1917 by the Treaty of Brest-Litovsk ('TR' 92). His policy, furthermore, of enslaving or exterminating those peoples who happened to occupy the territories which he had marked out as Germany's future 'living-space' would have been unthinkable to any earlier German leader, Trevor-Roper maintains. Taylor replies that this is to confound the pre-war Hitler with what he later became: he had no such policies in advance.[24] As for going beyond previous German territorial ambitions, Taylor sees him as, in some respects, actually more moderate than his predecessors ('T' 23). For in the First World War, the secret aims endorsed by the German Foreign Office included, not only Poland and the Ukraine, but also Belgium and parts of northern France. By contrast, Hitler sought, at most, expansion in the East; his war with the West was a mistake.

Now, as before, our question is not who is right or wrong, but why these historians, in trying to determine the causes of the Second World War, think it worthwhile to argue in these ways. It seems to me that their differences reveal a paradigm of causal thinking which is quite as familiar as the one we previously looked at. The general idea is that of causes as conditions which disrupt, or interfere with, or intrude upon, a settled state of affairs; or conversely, which restrict, or impede ongoing processes or movements. Thus a storm is said to be the cause of widespread flooding because it upsets normal patterns of drainage, and the presence of metal scrap in a piece of machinery is said to be the cause of its grinding to a halt because that is the relevant abnormality in the situation. As actually argued out, the historical case, too, often turns on perceptions of what is normal and abnormal.

Trevor-Roper sees Hitler as the intrusive, disturbing element in the international situation of the thirties; Taylor sees the disturbing elements elsewhere. The one thus ascribes to Hitler a causal role; the other refuses it. Clearly, although there is disagreement here about which of the various conditions of the war is to be identified as its cause, there is no disagreement about the criterion on which such identification should proceed. And this criterion is such that, in appealing to it, the first paradigm is completely transcended. It is true that Hitler's aims remain an issue; but what matters is no longer whether he was aiming at war. What matters is whether, whatever he was aiming at, and *even* if he was aiming at war, his having the aims he had, and his seeking to realize them in the ways he did, was normal or abnormal.

Obviously, unless there is something that can be taken as 'the normal state of affairs', no causal conclusion can be reached on such a paradigm. And if there are differences over the conception of normality to be applied, causal disagreements will sometimes be traceable as much to these differences as to any disagreement about what events occurred. Trevor-Roper sees this very clearly; and he accuses Taylor, in effect, of applying a standard of normality that is inappropriate to the situation he has in view. In regarding Hitler's aims and ambitions as normal, he complains, Taylor seems to be taking as his 'datum' for such judgments the position Germany enjoyed at the height of her success in the First World War, when she was 'victorious in the West and triumphant in the East' ('TR' 90). Anything less — for example, the Versailles settlement — is castigated as 'artificial' or 'unnatural'. Trevor-Roper himself seems to regard that settlement as providing a quite acceptable standard of normality for international relations in the thirties. There is evidence also of disagreement between the two historians about what counts as normal and abnormal in a more general sense. Thus, while Taylor is inclined to buttress his claim that Hitler's foreign policy was normal, even if self-aggrandizing, with the reflection that 'powers will be powers', Trevor-Roper tends to reject this line of apology. In fact, whether the issue is what was normal for German statesmen, in particular, given their national tradition, or what was normal for post-Versailles Europe in general, given its historical origins, or even what was normal for great powers as such, given the exigencies of a 'balance of power' world, the historians concerned seem quite ready to differ about it. And when they do, their causal conclusions differ too.

I cannot attempt here to analyse in any depth the logic of such judgments of normality. The point I would emphasize is simply how difficult it would be to maintain that the 'datum'[25] which they so evidently require is determinable objectively by the historian, in the sense of not requiring of him any value-judgments. Once a 'datum' has been decided upon, the determination of what is normal and abnormal may be largely a factual — perhaps even a statistical — matter. But the determination of what 'datum' would be appropriate in a particular inquiry surely is not. In fact, what often lies behind the judgments of normality lying behind the judgments of causality made by Taylor and many of his critics, appears to be a fundamental *political* value-judgment: a conception of what it was legitimate, politically speaking, to expect from Germans, post-Versailles Europeans, or great powers generally, in the twenties and thirties. I think it is significant, in this connection, that Taylor finds it relevant, in support of his own causal diagnosis, to remark that the Treaty of Versailles 'lacked moral validity from the start', and quite natural that Trevor-Roper should see this as a claim to be contested (even if Taylor does repudiate it in its fully normative sense in his 'Second Thoughts' ('T' 52, 7)). Also significant is Taylor's charge that the morality of Hitler's enemies was 'the morality of the *status quo*' ('T' 100). Britain and Poland, especially, he says (employing just the right degree of moral innuendo), were 'profiteers' from the First World War; their statesmen wanted the world to 'stand still as it had been created in 1919' ('T' 279). What gave these men's actions and attitudes their causal status, then, was their impeding developments that should have been accepted as normal and natural — the latter, it seems, at least partly because they were so reasonable.

## V

Paradigm three, I shall argue, goes in a similarly normative direction in the end. It has its origin, however, in the apparently innocuous idea that causes, since they are what *make* things happen, must be 'forcing' or 'active' conditions. Trevor-Roper evinces his acceptance of this idea especially in passages where he is rejecting what he considers the overly 'passive' view of Hitler which Taylor's account often presents — a feature which has been noted by many critics. Hitler is said to have been a 'master in the art of waiting' ('T' 300). He 'liked others to do his work for him' ('T' 142), seldom making demands himself, but simply acceding, more or less graciously, when what he wanted was dropped 'into his lap' ('T' 217). By contrast, opponents like Chamberlain were 'determined to start something' ('T' 172), and even subordinates like von Papen are said to have set 'the ball rolling' ('T' 181).[26] What is ascribed to Hitler in many of such passages, however, often goes beyond mere passivity. The German Führer is pictured, not only as failing to take the initiative himself, but as being forced continually to respond to the initiatives of others. He is manoeuvred, induced, incited, and even driven ('T' 189) to act by events and situations not of his own making.

Thus, according to Taylor, it was the Austrian Nazis, not Hitler, who first raised a storm about the *Anschluss*; and it was the Austrian Chancellor von Schuschnigg who, in spite of all Hitler's efforts to avoid a crisis, virtually compelled him to intervene by his decision to hold a plebiscite on the question of union, the circumstances being such that Germany could hardly have accepted the affront of a negative vote ('T' 8, 185-6). In the case of Czechoslovakia, it was similarly the Sudeten Germans, not Hitler, who took the initiative; Hitler simply concurred in a solution imposed by the British and French ('T' 8, 202-3). Later, when he occupied Prague, contrary to the agreement reached at Munich, Hitler was still only doing what he was forced to do – this time by the chaos that was spreading through the rump Czech state, inviting intervention by the Hungarians, whom the Germans had to anticipate ('T' 8, 248-9). In the case of Poland, far from showing aggressiveness, Hitler in fact showed remarkable restraint ('T' 203). He would have liked to settle peacefully and amicably the only outstanding issue between the two countries: the relatively minor question of Danzig ('T' 265 ff.). But he was hurried by the clamour of the local German population, alternately threatened and encouraged by the British, and, in the end, driven to desperate measures by the intransigence of the Polish premier, Beck, who refused even to negotiate. In none of these cases did Hitler initially set out to do what he eventually did; in all of them, according to Taylor, it was others who placed him in a position where he finally had to act.[27] The cause of what ensued was therefore not what he did himself; it was what was done by those who put him in that unfortunate position, and whose own actions were not similarly forced.

Trevor-Roper and other critics deny that the evidence will support such a view of a merely 'responding' Hitler ('TR' 95). It simply is not true, they say, that the German nationalist movements in Austria, Czechoslovakia, and Danzig were free of manipulation from Berlin – witness Hitler's appointment of the Sudeten leader as his 'Viceroy' (mentioned by Taylor himself ('T' 192)), and the way the German press, which was state-controlled, incited the dissidents in Danzig to revolt. And although Hitler did sometimes take advantage of situations he had not himself created, it is surely grotesque to say, in most cases, that he was *forced* to do what he did. The way Taylor contrives to give the contrary impression has seemed to many, indeed, nothing short of perverse. We are told, for example, that after the *Anschluss*, 'geography and politics automatically put Czechoslovakia on the agenda' ('T' 190). As P.A. Reynolds remarks sourly: they would hardly have done so 'had there not been in Berlin a government determined to destroy her'[28] – and we may presume that his point is not just that the existence of that government was also a necessary

condition of what ensued. As for the 'restraint' Hitler is alleged to
have shown over Poland, G.F. Hudson voices a common reaction
when he likens it to the 'restraint' of a bank-robber who hopes 'that
his victim may hand over the cash without resisting'.[29] A whole host
of Taylor's descriptions of actions and events have been seen in a
similar way: for example, his observation that, in the final crisis, when
one more round of diplomatic activity might have averted war by
splitting the British and the Poles, Hitler unfortunately could do
nothing, being 'a prisoner of his own timetable' ('T' 333). Still another
example is Taylor's claim that, in the second stage of the dismember-
ment of Czechoslovakia, the initiative, and hence also the point of
causal origin, lay not with Hitler, but with President Hacha, because,
instead of waiting to be summoned to Berlin, he actually asked for
an interview ('T' 9, 249–50).[30]

To say the least, Taylor's descriptions of Hitler as essentially passive,
or as merely responding, often seem somewhat value-laden. As before,
however, our concern is less with the correctness of what either he or
his critics have had to say than with the relevance of what they say
to the causal conclusions they draw; and, even more clearly than was
the case with examples falling under paradigm two, I think the value-
load can be seen to be directly relevant. It is functional, not orna-
mental. For the question whether or not Hitler was 'forced' to act,
in the sense at issue in the dispute, doesn't concern his psychological
powers of resistance, or his degree of bodily control. Nor is the
question whether he was 'active' or 'passive' the question whether
his actions were intentional or deliberate, and still less whether he
performed any actions at all. What is at issue is the sorts of reasons
there were for doing what Hitler did – the degree of justification he
had for claiming that, in view of the situations confronting him, vital
interests were in danger which it would be reasonable and proper to
defend, and which he therefore 'had' to defend. In other words, it is
a matter of the moral nature of the choices that were open to him –
so that, in a way structurally similar to what was observed in the case
of paradigm two, behind the judgments of activity and passivity that
lie behind the causal judgments lie value-judgments, indeed moral
judgments, about human life and action. Most of Taylor's critics simply
do not find it morally plausible to picture von Schuschnigg or Beck
as having left Hitler no reasonable alternative but to invade their
countries; or Hitler himself, given the momentous consequences of his
decisions, as having had no reasonable alternative but to follow his
own timetable. Trevor-Roper, in particular, rejects both Hitler's own
assessment of what counted as an unreasonable threat to vital interests,
and Taylor's implied agreement with it. In doing so, he resists also the
characterization of Hitler as merely responding to the initiatives of
others, and hence as being only part of the process by which, not he,

but they, brought on the war. It was Hitler's opponents, Trevor-Roper wants to say, who were put in the position of having to respond. It was Hitler who, in the relevant sense, provided the 'active' element.[31]

The moral oddity of much of Taylor's causal analysis comes out most strongly in what he has to say about the causal roles of those agents who provided Hitler with *opportunities* to advance from strength to strength. If Hitler occasionally seized an advantage, we seem to be told, the cause of any resulting harm is never to be sought in him; it is to be sought always in the blunders of those who allowed him to go on his escalating way. This suggests a rather different picture from that of the beleaguered leader forced to respond to pressures from all sides, and it seems doubtful that it can be fully subsumed under what I have called the third paradigm: for one thing, causes now become conditions which 'let' rather than 'make' things happen.[32] But if still another, a *fourth paradigm* must be recognized at this point, it is important to see that arguments which accord with it are similar to those we have just been examining in one crucial respect. They involve *a shift of the moral onus*.

In effect, Taylor views European statesmen of the thirties, other than Hitler, as having had, by virtue of their positions and powers, the task of identifying and neutralizing such threats to peace as Hitler represented. It should have been clear to them, Taylor apparently believes, that Hitler would take advantage of any opportunities he found for harm in this direction. These opportunities, therefore, ought not to have been provided. Since they *were* provided, and were in fact exploited, the cause of the harm that resulted must be traced to those who made it possible. This is the line of thinking that expresses itself, for example, in Taylor's observing that, as victors in the First World War, it was the British and French, not the Germans, who 'had the decision in their hands' ('T' 9, 270); and again in his declaring that, since certain opportunities for German aggrandizement envisaged in the Hossbach Memorandum did not after all materialize, we must 'look elsewhere for the man who provided an opportunity that Hitler *could* take, and who thus gave the first push towards war' — Chamberlain being 'an obvious candidate for this position' ('T' 172). To say the least, the active verb 'to push' here somewhat jars the ear, as do some other uses of it by Taylor to similar effect.[33]

What is especially strange about this whole form of argument, however, given the presumed aims of Taylor's revisionist work as a whole, is that it achieves its effect by treating Hitler as if he were quite outside the moral community. He is depicted as if he were some destructive force of nature, something merely *given*, something only to be guarded against — or, at most, as a mere reactive mechanism (Taylor notes that, when von Schuschnigg called the plebiscite, 'Hitler responded as though someone had trodden on a painful corn' ('T' 185)).

It is hard to believe that this is the way Taylor really wants us to regard him, in the end. For his determined attempt to display the Nazi leader as 'a normal German statesman' would seem to commit him rather to bringing Hitler back *into* the moral community. Taylor has been criticized for overdoing it; for emphasizing too much the rational in Hitler and ignoring the daemonic. But if a degree of re-habilitation, or at any rate of re-humanization, is indeed his intention, he can hardly, in consistency, present Hitler to us as caused to act by his own opportunities.

A further strangeness, of course, given the whole gamut of cases which seem so clearly to manifest the value-structured paradigms of causal reasoning that I have been discussing, is that Taylor himself apparently believes that, in elaborating his new interpretation of the causal significance of Hitler for the Second World War, he makes no value-judgments at all — none, at any rate, of the moral sort we have had chiefly in view. 'I do not come to history as a judge', he writes; ' . . . when I speak of morality I refer to the moral feelings at the time I am writing about. I make no moral judgments of my own' ('T' 7). According to Taylor, indeed, 'it is no part of a historian's duty to say what ought to have been done. His sole duty is to find out what was done and why' ('T' 26). One can only reply that the moral judgments which can be found covertly at work in his own causal reasoning show that he is mistaken so far as his own practice is concerned. And, in any case, *The Origins of the Second World War* is replete with moral judgments of the most overt, and even gratuitous kinds. We are told, for example, that the Munich agreement was 'a triumph for all that was best and most enlightened in British life' ('T' 7-8, 235); that the outcry against Stresemann after his death was 'grotesquely unjustified' ('T' 78); that the fear of the Italian navy by British admirals was 'a craven opinion' ('T' 125); that the rise of Fascism 'permanently debased the spirit of international affairs' ('T' 140). These are all judgments made by Taylor on his own authority; he is not simply relaying to us 'the moral feelings at the time'.

The point that most needs emphasizing, however, is that 'the moral feelings at the time' would not provide the historian with the selective principles he needs if he is to claim to discover what the causes of past events *really were* — assuming that he wishes to distinguish (as Taylor evidently does) between causes and mere conditions. If Taylor took his own precept seriously, the most he could consistently aim at would be an account of what the causes *seemed to be* from the standpoint of the various participants. In the case of the Second World War, we should learn only what the causes were from the standpoint of the Germans, British, French, Poles, Czechs, Russians and so on. In fact, Taylor offers us his own diagnosis (as he should), and in doing so, makes various value-judgments of his own. It might be noted that it has not always been his view that historians ought not to make value-judgments in the course of their work. In *Rumours of Wars*,[34] for example, while attacking Herbert Butterfield's advocacy of 'technical history', he takes a very different line. Although accepting Butterfield's admonition to historians to avoid 'moral fervour', he rebels against the notion that they should remain objective at the price of confining themselves to judging the past by the standards of the original agents. The historian, Taylor insists, cannot hope in such a way to avoid 'moral concerns'.[35] What he seems not to see, however, is that one of the reasons why this may be true is that the task (as he puts it himself) is 'to find out what was done and why'. For finding this out may require distinguishing between causes and mere conditions.

## VI

I have argued that there are at least four paradigms of causal attribution in the dispute between Taylor and his critics: four different concepts of what makes explanatory conditions distinctively causal. Since the first of these was conceded to be limited in scope — it being a truism that history is largely concerned with unintended consequences — and the others may be looked at askance by some because they are quasi-normative,[36] it is a matter of some importance to ask whether still further paradigms of causal thinking may not be discernible in what Taylor and his critics have to say. In fact, it is not too difficult to find implicit in Taylor's own work at least one further paradigm — this showing itself less clearly in the actual historical account he offers than in certain theoretical remarks he makes from time to time, Taylor being unusual among historians for the readiness with which he indulges in such remarks (his dicta on moral judgment in history being a case in point). What I shall refer to as the *fifth paradigm* is visible also, at least as an issue, in the reactions of some of Taylor's critics, especially those of a more theoretical orientation — for example, E.B. Segal and F.H. Hinsley. There are traces of it also, however, in the response of Trevor-Roper, and I shall therefore begin by drawing attention to some of these.

In discussing paradigm two, I noted the stress Trevor-Roper placed on such ideas as 'natural weight', 'artificiality', and 'calculation of reality' in his interpretation of Taylor's causal diagnosis. These I interpreted as quasi-evaluative; but another interpretation is certainly possible, and is in fact sometimes suggested by what Trevor-Roper himself says when formulating what he takes to be Taylor's view. Thus, having noted the causal significance claimed by Taylor for the fact that Germany, after Versailles, was 'still potentially the greatest power in Europe, naturally tending to revert to the 'real' position of January 1918', Trevor-Roper adds the gloss: 'All that intelligent German statesmen had to do . . . was to work hand-in-glove with this "historical necessity" – to their profit. All that Allied statesmen could do was to yield to the same necessity – to their loss' ('TR' 90). Elsewhere he ascribes to Taylor the view that the nature of the post-war settlement made the recovery of Germany's natural weight 'inevitable' ('TR' 96). And Taylor does indeed talk the language of inevitability at times, especially when speculating on what he refers to as the 'profound' causes of the war by contrast with the 'specific events' which led to it. This Trevor-Roper resists adamantly: it is men who make history, he says, not situations or states of affairs – men who have at least a degree of freedom of choice about what will occur ('TR' 90).[37] But he does not reject *as such* the idea of historical causes as what render certain results inevitable. He argues only that, in this further sense, Taylor fails to identify any plausible causes of the Second World War.

To put it a bit more formally, the conceptual framework for this further phase of the dispute seems to be the notion of a cause as a condition which is *sufficient* for its effect, or perhaps a set of conditions which are jointly so. Such a paradigm of causal connection is different from all of the others we have looked at in a very important respect. All of the latter, although each in a different way, required the contrast of one or a few necessary conditions with others which, although equally necessary for what occurred, were not themselves properly called its causes. The notion of cause as sufficient condition, on the contrary, involves – indeed, permits – no such contrast. There is thus no room in it for those normative considerations that were relevant in at least three of the other cases, these having come in only as grounds for distinguishing causes from mere conditions. Precisely for this reason, some may feel that here at last we have to do with a conception of causal connection which is appropriate to history as a discipline with some scientific pretensions, and hence with some obligation to seek value-free explanations. I have no wish, in the present context, to challenge this position directly, either as a statement of a certain ideal of historical inquiry, or as an expression of a certain conception of what causal connection might involve. I do, however, want to call attention to the extraordinarily heavy weather Taylor and his critics make of their efforts to find some concrete role for sufficient condition causes in the present dispute.

A major problem for understanding how Taylor himself conceives the role of causes of this sort is implicit in a central idea of the historical theory he sometimes applies to his own work. Taylor talks as if he believes that history is, and ought to be, written on two levels: a level at which a causal story is told in terms of the actions of individuals and the reasons they had for acting as they did; and another, a 'deeper' level, at which the historian lays bare those more 'profound' or 'underlying' causes to which I alluded a moment ago ('T' 42, 135 ff.). Taylor has been criticized for offering a rather perfunctory account of the war's profound causes;[38] and those he mentions — for example, the breakdown of the League of Nations, the glorification of war inherent in fascist regimes, a crisis of overproduction driving Germany to seek new markets, the prospect of a movement of the whole world balance against her as Russia and America gradually ended their isolation — are often mentioned only to be put in question ('T' 135 ff., 266 ff.). He frankly admits, however, that, as a diplomatic historian, his own interest is, in any case, in the first of the two levels. And what is more significant, although insisting on the importance of always remembering that the underlying causes exist, he is inclined to regard the level at which he himself prefers to work as *autonomous*, this justifying his relative neglect of the more profound causes. What his own narrative offers us by way of a first level account tends, in fact, as I have already indicated, to select as causes the policies and actions of individuals other than Hitler — at any rate, in its more polemical moods. In its more considered ones, it often depicts the coming of the war as a 'chapter of accidents' — 'the result on both sides of diplomatic blunders' ('T' 269) — this view reaching a kind of culmination in a much-quoted 'parting shot' of Taylor's book: that Hitler finally 'became involved in war through launching on 29 August a diplomatic manoeuvre which he ought to have launched on 28 August' ('T' 336).

Taylor pushes his thesis of the autonomy of causal explanation in diplomatic history to the point of claiming that it offers all the scope for significant individual action and human freedom that anyone — even a Trevor-Roper — could wish.[39] It is only at the second level that historical laws operate and historical inevitability sets in. That is, the two-level theory is conceived as affording a structure within which historians can be libertarians and determinists at the same time, and within which they can offer different, but compatible and non-competing explanations. In fact, Taylor often seems, in this connection, to confuse an *accidental* theory of history with an *indeterminist* one. To argue that the Second World War was due, even in a fairly minor way, to Hitler's bad timing, is not to argue that the actions of any of the relevant individuals, including Hitler, lacked determining conditions. For all Taylor's accidental view implies to the contrary, there could be explanations of a fully deterministic sort for all of them. Many might nevertheless argue that causal explanation on paradigm three, at least — a kind that Taylor's diplomatic history characteristically employs — requires the assumption of human free will and a denial of a complete determinism in history; for in requiring an appraisal of the moral nature of the choices of the agents involved, it surely implies that they had a genuine choice. It might be held, too, that explanation on paradigms one and two are at least *compatible* with indeterministic assumptions. A certain spectre therefore remains: the possibility that historians working at different levels may give causal explanations of the same events which are *in*compatible, and hence radically competing ones.

When we turn from Taylor's theorizing back to relevant examples of his practice and to the reactions of his critics, however, other alternatives suggest themselves. One such, which is the direct contrary of the possibility that we have just noted, is that first-level causes are themselves to be explained deterministically by second-level ones, the diplomatic story then having to be seen as just the 'way' the profound causes worked themselves out. This seems to be the view ascribed to Taylor by E.B. Segal when he says that the admission of an underlying 'geopolitical reality', which changes in accordance with 'inevitable laws', requires Taylor to admit that the decisions and policies of human agents 'could not "logically" have been any different from what they were'.[40] In fact, I don't myself find Taylor ever arguing this way. A variation on the same doctrine which is a bit more plausible, because looser, and which is attributed to Taylor by Trevor-Roper, is that human intelligence is best employed in 'allowing' events to 'conform' to 'objective realities', since these realities otherwise 'have to assert themselves at greater human cost, through the mess caused by human blunders' ('TR' 90).

More characteristic of Taylor, I think, is a renunciation, not of the belief in upper-level indeterminism, but of any claim that the profound causes were themselves sufficient conditions of the war. This is done, however, in a variety of ways. One is to hold that what the profound causes were sufficient for is not the war, but only certain things falling short of it, such as the return of Germany to power, and perhaps her challenging her former enemies in some way ('T' 65). Often when it may seem that Taylor is citing conditions that made *the war* inevitable, he is really defending only some such lesser thesis – as Trevor-Roper represents him as doing in the passage I quoted about the inevitability of Germany's regaining her 'natural weight'. A second alternative is to regard the profound causes as rendering the outbreak of war itself, not certain, but only probable – this sometimes being reduced to 'possible' ('T' 136). Thus, as Taylor's doctrine is summarized by F.H. Hinsley: international anarchy (one of Taylor's profound causes), while not invariably producing war, does 'invariably tend to invite it'.[41] Still a third possibility is to hold that what the profound causes made inevitable was *either* war *or* some specified alternative – as when Taylor declares that after Versailles, 'the only question was whether the settlement would be revised and Germany become again the greatest power in Europe peacefully or by war' ('T' 79). Still a fourth possibility is that what the profound causes did was make the war inevitable *unless* certain things were done to prevent it — as when Taylor, having said that the Second World War was 'implicit' in the ending of the First, wonders whether it might not have been averted nevertheless, either by 'greater firmness or by greater conciliation' on the part of the Western Allies ('T' 336).

It seems, therefore, that although Taylor retains in theory the concept of cause as sufficient condition, and perhaps even claims from time to time to know conditions which are sufficient for some other things, he doesn't actually claim to know any profound causes of the war itself which are sufficient conditions of it. Yet he claims to know some profound causes of the war. He thus abandons the fifth paradigm so far as the causal explanation of the war is concerned: he recognizes two kinds of causes, at two different levels, but sees neither as consisting in more than necessary conditions of what is caused. If that is the situation, however, we need to ask in what sense Taylor can go on talking of two autonomous levels of causal inquiry. If the profound causes do not explain the occurrence of the war without the particular ones, or the particular ones without the profound, how can we really speak of having two different, but compatible, levels of explanation? Isn't what we have really two parts of a single explanation which recognizes the necessity of both certain predisposing conditions and the actions of certain individuals? The conclusion which suggests itself, in fact, is that historians working at the diplomatic and geopolitical levels simply make different selections from a single set of explanatory conditions — perhaps on no more significant criterion than that certain conditions happen to interest them more than others. On such a view, the only reason Taylor could have for saying that what caused the war was, say, Chamberlain's policies rather than the loss by Germany of her 'natural weight' is that he happens to be doing diplomatic history. Actually, this is uncomfortably close to what Taylor himself does sometimes say.

Hinsley, at least, will not let Taylor retreat unchallenged into such a policy of historiographical 'live and let live'. Hinsley regards it as beyond dispute that both certain predisposing conditions, notably the 'acute international unbalance' after Versailles, and the policies of certain statesmen, notably Hitler, were involved in the outbreak of the Second World War, and need to be taken into account in explaining it. But 'the relationship between the given conditions and the policy of statesmen', he maintains, 'is not a constant and mechanical relationship . . . One war may be almost entirely due to the given conditions and hardly at all the consequence of the conduct of the men involved. Another war may be almost entirely due to that conduct'. What the historian must do is ask, in each case, what

91

'relative weight' should be assigned to 'the two levels of causation'.[42] It is Hinsley's contention that, in the case of the Second World War, the contributions of the men were quite crucial and the contributions of the conditions less so. 'It was practically impossible', he says, 'for other powers to resist Germany's revisionist attitude up to and including the Munich crisis'; but it was 'equally impossible that they should not resist if it were persisted in beyond that point'. Hitler did pursue his revisionism beyond the critical point; he refused 'to modify the policy of exploiting the unbalance for his ends'. 'It was this fact, not the unbalance itself, that caused the war.'

What we get in this critical response of Hinsley is not only a retreat from paradigm five, but a re-assertion of something like paradigms two or three. The implication is that if the war had come in response to Hitler's policies any time up to and including Munich, then Hitler could not have been said to have caused it. Whether in that case the cause would have been the unbalance itself or the responses of the other powers, Hinsley does not say. But the important point for present purposes is that, if Hitler's exploitation of the unbalance beyond the crucial point is to be seen as converting his policies from non-causal to causal status, this can only be on some criterion which distinguishes genuine causes from mere conditions. And the criteria actually employed seem to be those we have noted already. Hitler's demands in the later period are judged by Hinsley to have been 'excessive' — that is, they are seen as relevantly abnormal. Hinsley actually observes that Hitler's 'appetite for success' proved greater than is 'normal'.[43] By contrast, he regards Hitler's earlier demands as non-causal, since they were expressions of legitimate needs — that is, they were things that *had* to be done. Hinsley refuses either to say that one level of cause is by its very nature fundamental, or to renounce paradigm five just to offer an undifferentiated list of 'causal factors': mere necessary conditions subjected to no further analysis. Such a refusal is characteristic of a good deal of historical writing.


# VII


I remarked at the beginning that I could hardly aim, in the present compass, at elaborating a whole theory of the causal concept in history. In fact, what has been said hardly amounts to a *theory*, even of the distinction between causes and mere conditions as it functions in the present dispute. What has emerged is perhaps more accurately described as some of the data — some of the 'conceptual facts' — which any such theory ought to be prepared to take into account. To judge by this particular controversy, at any rate, historians regard conditions of at least the following five kinds as having special claim to be accorded causal status: those which were intended to bring about the result; those which interfered with normal processes or states of affairs; those which compelled or forced people to act; those which enabled or allowed things to happen or to be done; and (possibly) those which rendered what occurred inevitable — all but the first and last of these requiring the historian's own value-judgment in various ways. Such notions of what it is to be a cause are apparently taken seriously enough for historians to argue with each other in ways that presuppose their applicability. That isn't to say that the ideas themselves are crystal clear in what they typically have to say. What is at issue is guiding paradigms, not precise logical formulas. But the paradigms do seem to *function*.

Some will, of course, resist such claims, perhaps doubting that I have correctly caught the sense of what the various historians were arguing. I can only hope, in that case, that they will produce more defensible analyses of their own. But suppose that the above analysis is broadly correct, at least as an account of what was going on in this particular dispute. What questions next arise? By way of conclusion, let me mention two.

The first is what is to be made of the fact that the historians under study seem to be working with, not one, but a number of rather different notions of what makes a necessary condition a specifically causal one. One wonders whether these notions could not somehow be brought together into a single theory of the causal concept for history: whether, for example, all could not be shown to be derived from some more fundamental notion, or, at any rate, related to each other in some understandable way.[44] This question is given urgency by the fact that some paradigms appear to conflict with each other. For example, as was pointed out above, the fifth seems to make deterministic assumptions while the others may not. And even if the relating of the other four does not encounter that particular difficulty, any attempt at a general theory would have to face the problem that, at least sometimes, the latter yield at any rate different (and perhaps competing) causal judgments — a situation that the historians seem, at times, indeed, ready to exploit, switching paradigms at points where favoured causal theses begin to run into trouble. Thus, while, on the first paradigm, Hitler may have to be regarded as a cause of the war if he is agreed to have intended it in a relevant sense and to a sufficient degree, on the second, he may properly be judged not to have been a cause of it if his intentions, even including that one, are seen as normal by reference to appropriate standards of comparison. Similarly, while, on paradigm three, Chamberlain can hardly be considered to have been a cause, even by Taylor, since he did not actually force Hitler to act as he did, he may still have to be accorded causal status on paradigm four — as Taylor sometimes wants to do — if it can be shown that his policies nevertheless enabled Hitler to act.

There is the further peculiarity, noted towards the end of section V, that, as Taylor, at any rate, applies paradigm four, certain agents who, for the purpose of giving causal judgments on paradigm three, would naturally be considered responsible moral agents (they could not be 'forced' in the relevant sense if they were not), seem somewhat arbitrarily excluded from moral appraisal — as when Hitler is relegated to the mere background of what was occurring, as if he were a natural force. In discussing this point, I noted a certain *moral* oddity in Taylor's thesis; but what is perhaps more relevant to our analytical purposes is the *logical* oddity of his treating Hitler in the same historical work, and with respect to the same historical circumstances, both as morally responsible and as not morally responsible. Clearly there is much to investigate further here. It is conceivable that, in the practice of historians, implicit but coherent rules could be found for the use of one paradigm rather than another, and even for switching paradigms in certain contexts. But, at present, this can only be a speculation.

A second question that will doubtless arise for many out of what has been said is the following. Suppose it to have been shown that these particular historians allowed their causal inquiries to be guided by paradigms of the sort that have been elicited; suppose it to be the case, even, that the majority of historians proceed in this way. Are we to conclude from this that such procedures are *justifiable*? The philosopher of history doubtless has some responsibility to find out what is actually going on in the discipline about which he wishes to theorize; but surely he is not committed to accepting whatever he finds. Philosophy cannot just be descriptive, even if analytical; it must always pass over into appraisal and criticism. In view of the difficulties adumbrated, should we not perhaps conclude that much existing historiography is in dire need of reform? Might not the moral of the analysis be that historians should *give up* using causal concepts of at least the first four, value-impregnated kinds?

There are two observations that I should like to make on this. First, before saying too much about what historians ought to be doing, it is important to ask what purposes may be served by what they are doing already. So far as the present analysis goes, at any rate, it seems plausible to say that causal judgments made on paradigms one to four help to make the human past intelligible *as human affairs*: they help to give a human meaning to a human subject-matter. In fact, to echo and expand what was said at the end of the chapter on Collingwood, the concepts of cause embedded in these paradigms could appropriately be called 'humanistic'. They require for their application a perception of human agents as acting for reasons, and thus presuppose understanding of the Collingwoodian kind. They require also what might be called 'respect' for past human agents: a consideration of them in their full capacity as moral beings, and thus as acting in ways that invite judgment.[45] Although the concepts in question by no means exclude the selection of social events or processes as causes, they make it impossible simply to *ignore* the claims of human individuals to such status — as the arguments of Hinsley well illustrate. In fact, the case for calling a social, or even a physical, condition a cause will often consist, in part, of showing, by quasi-moral reasoning, why, in that particular case, the actions of certain individuals cannot be so regarded. It should be noted that such notions of what historical causes can or must be like are not the inventions of historians (or philosophers). They belong to very familiar ways of thinking about the world: ways in which those to whom historians wish to communicate their results will naturally think, and in which, indeed, it is difficult not to think. Historians who succeeded in renouncing them altogether would produce accounts that would scarcely be recognizable as history.

And this leads to my second observation. To put this in the form of a question: How else might historians proceed in inquiries which are aimed at discovering causes? Should they look only for sufficient conditions? It seems to be generally agreed that, in most historical cases, nothing very closely approximating the latter are to be found. Should they then aim at discovering only some of the necessary conditions of what they take as problematic — gradually filling out that list of mere causal 'factors' that Hinsley, for one, repudiated as a proper goal for historical inquiry? This may sound possible, at least; but what does it mean? Would the rejection of all criteria of causal selection implicit in paradigms one to four require us to conclude that, for purposes of causal diagnosis, one necessary condition is as good as another? That this leads to unacceptable results is most easily seen with reference to negative conditions, an indefinitely long list of which can easily be 'discovered' for any historical event simply by asking what, if it *had* happened, would have made a difference to the result, its not happening then being designated a cause of what in fact happened. The triviality in which such a procedure could land an inquiry might be illustrated by the identification of the 'failure' of the leaders of the Nazi regime simultaneously to suffer cardiac arrest on the evening of 31 August 1939 (this surely would have 'made a difference'), as a cause of the outbreak of the war the next day. Yet it would be extravagant to try to avoid such problems (as Mandelbaum would apparently do[46]) by denying causal status entirely to negative conditions. The failure of British and French politicians (a real failure this time) to see what Hitler was driving at until it was too late surely ought not to be ruled out of consideration as a likely cause of the eventual outbreak of war on any such arbitrary principle.

Would it be possible instead, then, while retaining the distinction between necessary conditions (including negative ones) which are causes and those which are not, to draw the distinction between them on criteria which, if not entirely value-free, are at least free of moral considerations — the aspect of present practice most likely to bother critics. This is a possibility that should certainly be explored; but it remains to be seen whether it can be done in a way that retains any significant contact with the causal judgments we are, in fact, inclined to make. Meantime, causal concepts are to be seen at work in history, although admittedly not always tidily or even entirely consistently, that appear closely bound up with the task of making the past significant as human affairs. On the question of whether the latter should be rejected for something else, the burden of proof surely lies with those who propose reform.

# Part Three

# V   A Vision of World History: Oswald Spengler and the Life-Cycle of Cultures

## I

Up to this point, the focus of discussion has been on some major problems of 'critical' philosophy of history: that is, philosophy of history in the sense of an analysis of the concepts and assumptions of historical knowledge and inquiry. I turn finally to consider the views of an author whose main concerns lie within what is generally called 'speculative' philosophy of history: an inquiry not into the arguments and procedures of historians, but into the nature of the historical process itself. Of course, historians, too, study the historical process; but speculative philosophers of history endeavour to study it in a sense, or at a level, which drives them far beyond the piecemeal reconstructions that are characteristic of ordinary historical work. Indeed, what they aim at transcends even universal history, or history of the world — the sort of thing offered by great historical synthesizers such as H.G. Wells[1] or (more recently) W.H. McNeill.[2] What they try to achieve is an interpretation of universal history which will abstract from the whole human past something that might be called 'the meaning of it all'. Perhaps the best-known modern example of the speculative enterprise, thus conceived, is the work of the historian-turned-philosopher, Arnold Toynbee.[3] The author whose doctrines I shall be examining in this chapter, Oswald Spengler, to some extent anticipates Toynbee's methods and conclusions, as he acknowledges himself. However, the spirit and style of the two constructions are very different — that of Spengler being, from a theoretical standpoint at least, in many ways the more interesting.

I used the word 'author' in referring to Spengler because it is hard to characterize him in any more specific way. Unlike other major philosophical writers on history — for example, Kant or Hegel — and

99

unlike Collingwood and Watkins among the critical theorists we considered earlier, Spengler has no general reputation as a philosopher: in fact, he produced no other philosophical writing of substance besides the book for which he is known, *The Decline of the West*.[4] Again unlike Collingwood, although in this case like most other speculative philosophers of history, Spengler himself did no significant original historical research; his historical knowledge is all second hand. However, he had read widely, if somewhat erratically, and he has generally been hailed for his 'erudition'. Politically he was an ardent German nationalist, and he made no bones about this in his writing. His extreme right-wing views, with a tendency to talk rather wildly at times about the importance of 'race' and 'blood' (I, 113 ff.), have led some to regard him as the philosopher of history *par excellence* of Fascism — by contrast, for example, with Marx as the philosopher of history of Communism, and (some might say) Toynbee as the philosopher of history of liberalism.[5] In fact, although he seems to have been in sympathy with Hitler's nationalist aims, Spengler was quickly disillusioned by the Nazis, who eventually took measures against him. In any case, his German nationalism is easily separated from his larger views of history, and can be virtually ignored in trying to understand his overall system.

*The Decline of the West* was published in two volumes in the early 1920s, and it brought Spengler almost instant fame, rapidly selling 100,000 copies — this, despite its formidably oracular style, apparent lack of organization and exhausting prolixity (one commentator, H. Stuart Hughes, has described it as a typical expression of the traditional German conviction that if a book is worth writing, it is worth making difficult to read[6]). At least part of the explanation for Spengler's initial success was doubtless the readiness of the German market for some kind of reflection on 'decline' after the defeat of 1918.[7] But the thesis that Western culture was *in general* in decline also appealed to many outside Germany in the 1920s, as it did again after the Second World War, when Spengler's ideas enjoyed another brief period of popularity. Others have simply found his book fascinating, in spite of its obscurity — often while claiming to reject most of its arguments. Thus Northrop Frye describes it as 'German romanticism at its corniest', full of 'Halloween imagery' and 'woowoo noises' about 'the dark goings-on of nature and destiny';[8] but he confesses that, as a young man, he slept with it under his pillow for several years — an impressive sign of addiction given the fact that the English translation runs to almost a thousand pages. The Dutch historian J.H. Huizinga too, typically finds Spengler quite often 'absurd'; yet he acknowledges himself also, at times, 'bewitched' by him; 'he compels us', he says, 'to forget that we know better.'[9] In outlining Spengler's theory, I shall make use of enough of his own phrases to allow the reader to begin to form some judgment on this matter for himself.

## II

A few words should be said, first, about Spengler's general approach. It is sometimes suggested by friendly critics that, although his theory may be unacceptable as a whole, what Spengler has to say, in elaborating his views, is nevertheless full of valuable 'insights'. It is important to be clear, therefore, that *The Decline of the West* does not claim just to convey a collection of insights; it claims, as Spengler himself puts it, to 'predetermine' history (I, 3). That is, it claims to provide us with an analysis that will justify historical prediction, and this on a very grand scale. Spengler insists, in fact, that he is the first thinker to have provided a sound basis for doing any such thing.

The first requisite for an approach of this kind to historical studies, he says, is that we abandon the common practice of regarding the historical past as a progression from the ancient to the medieval to the modern world. This *linear* view of history, which he calls 'incredibly jejune' (I, 16), is Europe-centred. It is a view of the human past which, according to Spengler, is reminiscent of the Ptolemaic, earth-centred view of the *physical* universe which was overturned by Copernicus in the sixteenth century (I, 18). What is needed in historical inquiry, he avers, is a new Copernican revolution. And with what Hughes has called his 'characteristic lack of modesty',[10] he presents himself as the new Copernicus (I, 25). What was important about the original Copernican revolution, it must be remembered, was not simply its substituting the sun for the earth as the centre of the celestial system. It was rather its opening the way for the abandoning of all thought of a centre at all. In history, too, Spengler insists, we must learn to see our object of study as having no centre, no focus, no single point of reference.

What can be said, then, about the whole human past from the Copernican point of view? Spengler's answer could be put, I think, as responses to three large, inter-related questions that almost any speculative philosophy of history would try to answer. The first is what overall *pattern* can be discovered in the events of human history. The second is what explains the *formation* of this pattern — what productive 'mechanism' is responsible for it, why it came about. The third is what *meaning* or *significance* can be attributed to human history as a whole if it has this pattern and mechanism — for example, what value or purpose it can be said to achieve. A linear philosophy of history like Hegel's[11] responds to the first of these questions by tracing a progressive social development from the ancient oriental empires, through periods of Persian, Greek and Roman domination, down to the rise of the Western or 'Germanic' world. To the second question, it gives the rather mysterious, and certainly highly metaphysical answer, that 'Reason' has been at work in the historical process, cunningly exploiting human passions for worth-while ends of which the agents themselves were generally quite unaware. And to the third, it replies that there has been achieved, through this process, a degree of human freedom and a level of human spirituality which could not have come about in any other way. The way Spengler answers the same three questions is, briefly, as follows.

Using a technique which he calls, somewhat grandly, 'comparative morphology' (I, 50, 111–13), he reaches the conclusion that the pattern of the past is the story of the careers of a number of large social units which he calls cultures, one of these being Western society of the present day. These cultures are born, grow, mature and die 'with the same superb aimlessness as the flowers of the field' (I, 21). Like flowers, they have a species similarity, and a natural life-span. But unlike flowers, they have no parent–offspring relation with each other; each is an independent growth (here Spengler's theory is quite unlike Toynbee's, which traces a genealogy of civilizations through three generations). Nor do Spengler's cultures (as do Toynbee's) have significant relations of other kinds with each other: for example, they do not influence, or even genuinely stimulate each other. Thus, if there is any pattern in history, it must be sought, not in developments *between* the cultures, but in developments *within* them. Most of his book is devoted to describing such developments.

The second large question thus becomes, for Spengler, the question why the cultures develop internally as they do. His official answer is that each fulfils its own peculiar 'destiny' (I, 145–6). This certainly sounds obscure; but at least this much could be said by way of preliminary clarification. What Spengler appears to be working with here is a quasi-biological notion of a seed – in this case a cultural seed – as a mysterious source of life: something which, like an acorn or a hazel nut, can only develop in a predetermined way, and for whose distinctive pattern of development there is no ultimate explanation. Perhaps, one day, the science of biology will make such a notion of a living seed as something with a fixed and inexplicable 'destiny' an unnecessary, or even an unacceptable notion (indeed, we seem sometimes to be told that it has done so already). Our concern at this point, however, is with what Spengler *means*; and what he has to say about the destiny of a culture is certainly analogous to this still quite familiar way of thinking about the reproduction of living things.

Two kinds of investigation suggest themselves as appropriate to a subject-matter so conceived. First, we can ask in each case what kind of cultural seed we have to deal with.[12] To find the answer to this question, Spengler says, we need 'physiognomic tact' (I, 389; II, 4) — or, to put it more bluntly, a kind of historical intuition (with which Spengler himself claims to be unusually well endowed). Second, we can note the stages through which each cultural seed develops as it realizes its predestined nature, with a view to discovering, if possible, some pattern of normal development which will hold good for all cultures. Spengler claims, in fact, to find such a pattern, the details of which we shall consider presently. He endeavours also to account for discovered deviations from the supposed normal pattern in similarly quasi-biological terms. For example, he represents cultures as sometimes interfering with each other's development, just as plants do when they invade each other's ground or get in each other's light — a process which (this time drawing on mineralogy) he calls 'pseudo-morphosis' (II, 189). As in the case of plants, however, the resulting changes are said never to be more than external in nature. They never touch what is essential to a culture — just as, although an ivy may deform an oak, it can never change its essential nature.

Given answers such as these to the pattern and mechanism questions, what can be said about the meaning or significance of the whole human past? Spengler thinks it obvious that no meaning or significance at all can be found in history as a whole. Considered as a whole, what we should normally call the historical past is a formless expanse of human life within which centres of meaning or significance — that is, cultures — from time to time make an appearance and pass away. Spengler sometimes expresses this idea by saying that most of history is, in fact 'historyless' — a play on words that other speculative philosophers of history (for example, Marx) have indulged in for similar effect. There is thus an important sense in which, although the Spenglerian view of history centres on the rise and fall of cultures, it is not really a *cyclical* theory at all, although it is often classified as such.[13] There is no recurring pattern of events, each ending constituting a new beginning, as, for example, in the theories of Vico or Toynbee. Perhaps, for Spengler, history as a whole could be said to possess meaning or significance in the very attenuated sense of providing a vehicle — or, perhaps we should say seed-bed — for the sporadic realization of various possibilities of cultural growth. But that is all.

## III

Against the background of this sketch of Spengler's overall theory, let me now go on to expand on certain aspects of it. I shall look first, in a more detailed way, at what Spengler tells us about the general nature of the culture units; then at what he says about the distinctive nature of some of the historical cultures that he recognizes; then at his account of the typical career of a culture; and finally at the way he applies his analysis to the question that gave his theory its initial claim to fame: that of the future of the West.


## IV

As will not be surprising after what has just been said, Spengler is often accused of 'biologizing' history. Certainly he regards his cultures as 'organisms', and he constantly talks the language of organisms (I, 104). However, if his cultures are organisms, it is important to note that they are organisms of a peculiarly 'spiritual' kind, even if rooted in a 'mother-landscape' (I, 174). By this I mean that they consist essentially in a basic *attitude* or *orientation* to the world, which shows itself in all the activities of their members – their art, religion, economics, philosophy, politics, science, technology – even their modes of warfare and their amusements (I, 175). This basic orientation has to be intuited by the Spenglerian historian. And since what has to be intuited is, in fact, a matter of *style* (I, 174, 108), a certain *style of living in the world*, what lies at the foundation of the Spenglerian view of history is essentially a species of aesthetic judgments which the historian must be prepared to make. Spengler's theory is by far the most aesthetic of the great speculative systems. Hence, no doubt, its appeal to literary readers like Frye.

The aesthetic dimension of the theory becomes the plainer when Spengler goes on to tell us that the style of a culture is expressible in terms of a *prime symbol*. This symbol, always a spatial notion of some kind – a 'view of the Macrocosm' – reflects the way a culture conceives the world in which it has to live, and to which its style of life must therefore be appropriate. To give one or two examples: the prime symbol of Western culture, which Spengler (inspired by Goethe) calls 'Faustian', is *infinite extension*, or 'pure and limitless space' (I, 183). Thus, the life-style of Faustian man is characterized by ceaseless striving, as if he were trying to fill infinite space with his activities. By contrast, Classical man, Graeco-Roman man – lived in a world of the here-and-now, which he was content simply to enjoy. The space symbol of this culture, which Spengler (this time inspired by Nietzsche) calls 'Apollinian', is thus *local place*, or 'limited self-contained Body' (I, 174). Architectural expressions of the very different space symbols of these two cultures are the Gothic cathedral which 'soars', and the Greek temple which 'hovers' (I, 177). Intellectual expressions are Euclidean geometry, the mathematics of bounded space, and the calculus, the mathematics of infinite movement (I, 64, 75).

Other aspects of Western culture which Spengler regards as particular expressive of its Faustian spirit include perspective painting, the fugue (which explores infinite 'tonal space'), long-distance communications, long-range weapons, imperialism (Spengler quotes with relish the dictum of Cecil Rhodes: 'expansion is everything') and bureaucratic institutions which arise out of a 'feeling of care', the latter showing itself also in the ubiquitous Madonna-and-child theme of Western art (I, 7, 37, 136–7, 183, 333). Further aspects of Classical culture which are seen as especially revelatory of its basic orientation include a religion of local gods, a drama of situations rather than of character development, a sculpture of the life-sized human body (with 'no incorporeal *arrière-pensée* whatsoever'), the local politics of the city-state, the practice of burning rather than burying the dead (as if eternity were an unthinkable idea), no clocks, no predictive astronomy – and no history (I, 9, 15, 130, 176, 183, 188). This last may appear a strange judgment on a culture generally thought to have produced the Father of History himself. Spengler's point, however, is that the Greek historians confined themselves largely to contemporary history; they thus lacked what, for us (as was argued in chapter II, section II), is the most essential quality of an historian, namely 'perspective'. Thucydides, in particular, he says, reveals his complete 'lack of historical feeling', when, on the very first page of his book, he makes 'the astounding statement that before his time (about 400 BC) no events of importance had occurred' (I, 10). The fundamentally different attitudes of Classical and Faustian man towards 'the distant' are to be seen also, Spengler avers, in the way they treat 'relics' of the past. Faustians show 'a wistful regard' for ruins, and a passion to excavate and to exhibit. By contrast, while 'every Greek knew his "Iliad" . . . not one ever thought of digging up the hill of Troy' (I, 254).[14]

In all, Spengler claims to discern nine historic cultures, each with its own unique style of life expressible through a distinctive space symbol, although he would not deny that there may be others yet to be discovered. In fact, his knowledge of the ones he mentions is quite uneven – very much more so than Toynbee's of his somewhat comparable units. What he knows best, naturally enough, is the Faustian and Apollinian cultures. He has quite a bit to say about a third, which he calls 'Magian', and which he claims to have been the first to notice: a chiefly Arabian culture (although including a number of other Middle Eastern groups as well) whose career overlapped with those of the other two, and which they to a considerable extent deformed. Besides these three, he recognizes four ancient cultures, a Babylonian, a Chinese, an Egyptian and an Indian, which he barely mentions from time to time; a comparatively recent Mexican culture (also something of a rag-bag), which he concedes he knows next to nothing about; and an embryonic Russian culture which, according to him, has scarcely yet begun to live a life of its own, having suffered pseudomorphosis through repeated involvement with the West: for example, through the reforms of Peter the Great, the Europe-centred foreign policies of Alexander I, and the Bolshevik Revolution (II, 193, 195). Let me say just a word or two about the space symbols of some of these other cultures.

The Magian culture, according to Spengler, was a 'cavern' culture: its space symbol was a domed interior — an inside with only an implied outside (I, 200). Hence the mosque, and, in general, an interior-oriented architecture in which windows are purely functional, mere 'holes in the wall' (I, 199). Hence also a tendency towards magical, dualistic religions (Judaism, early Christianity, and Islam all being Magian, according to Spengler), full of contending powers of light and darkness, sacred books and rites (I, 183, 306, 363; II, 68). The Magian talent for *mystery* shows itself also in its 'sparkling, predominantly golden, mosaics and arabesques', which drown the cavern in an 'unreal, fairy-tale light' (gold, as an 'unnatural' colour, being superbly Magian); and in the practice of alchemy, with its claim to render transmutable what appears hard and irreducible (I, 200, 248, 382). This talent for mystery extends, in fact, even to the culture's most impressive intellectual achievement: the invention of algebra. For the latter, with its manipulation of 'indefinite' numbers is sheer hocus-pocus, at any rate by contrast with the mathematics of the Greeks (I, 72–3).

The Egyptian culture was a 'linear' one: it conceived of life as a rigidly prescribed journey towards a fated outcome — an inexorable movement in one-dimensional space towards the tomb (I, 189). Egyptian temples thus tend to be little more than 'a path enclosed by mighty masonry', and Egyptian statues lack depth, being meant to be looked at only from the front as one passes (I, 225, 202). Appropriately enough, Egyptian culture shares with the Faustian a strong historical sense and a 'feeling of care' (I, 12). The culture of the ancient Chinese was also linear; but its space symbol is a meandering pathway rather than a straight line; 'the Chinaman *wanders* through his world' (I, 190). How natural then, observes Spengler (with characteristic resourcefulness), that alone among the great peoples of the world, the ancient Chinese, conceiving life more or less as a stroll through a 'landscape', should have raised gardening to the status of a 'grand religious art' (I, 190). Finally, Spengler suspects that what is in process of gestation in Russia at the present time is a culture whose prime symbol will be a 'plane without limit' (I, 201). This appears already, he says, although scarcely with 'sure expression', in a native ethics of brotherhood rather than of striving, and a preference in matters architectural for low-lying buildings — at any rate, when the native genius is left undisturbed by the West (I, 309).

# V

Once having identified the basic culture units, comparative morphology can proceed with its second task, the discovery of the patterns of development *within* the cultures. When Spengler lines up his specimens for comparison, what he claims to find is that each culture has a natural life-span of about a thousand years, during which period all go through analogous stages of growth and decay. Indeed, he goes so far as to assert that 'there is not a single phenomenon of deep physiognomic importance in the record of one [culture] for which we could not find a counterpart in the record of every other . . . under a characteristic form and in a perfectly definite chronological position' (I, 112). This identical pattern he is inclined to represent as an *ageing process* — something like the passage of the human individual from youth to senility in roughly 'three-score years and ten' (I, 110). He likens it also, at times, to the succession of the seasons in nature — spring, summer, autumn, winter — the story being one of the maturation of a cultural style which eventually exhausts itself and dies a natural death.

Spengler does concede that the full pattern of growth and decay is not always realized. The Mexican culture, for example, did not die naturally; it was destroyed by invaders from the Faustian world when it was just past the zenith of its powers — and in an historical episode so 'cruelly banal, so supremely absurd', as to be almost sufficient in itself to show that the overall course of history can have 'no meaning whatever' (II, 44). Spengler's point is that what happened in this contact between two cultures — if, indeed, the arrival of a few Faustian adventurers could be called that — derived from no 'inner necessity' of either of them or of the relation between them. It has to be noted, too, that a culture can go on existing after the ageing process has run its course. Thus, according to Spengler, the Chinese and Indian cultures have lingered on as mere 'scrap material' of history for many centuries since their allotted life-span came to an end (I, 36). To change the metaphor, they now resemble 'worn-out giant(s) of the primeval forest [thrusting] their decaying branches to the sky' (I, 106). The crucial claim is that nothing of significance in a given cultural style ever occurs again, once the thousand years are up. Other cultures may live and grow on the same ground; but that is another matter.

Let me give a brief outline of the 'four seasons' idea as Spengler applies it to the Faustian and Apollinian cultures. Every spring begins in a Heroic Period, characterized by vital myths, mystical religion, epic poetry and spontaneous, if anonymous, art. These express a fresh, deeply-felt, but somewhat inchoate world-view which will only later receive intellectual elaboration. At this stage, the culture has an agricultural economy, a highly functional ruling class — 'primary classes' of nobility and priesthood (II, 96) — and strong territorial

107

roots. In the Apollinian culture, this was the Homeric period, from about 1100 BC. In the Faustian culture it was the Middle Ages, from about AD 900. Typical of the exact 'correspondences' which Spengler finds at this stage are those between Homer and the *Niebelungenlied*, and the 'Trojan War' and the Crusades (I, 27). It is a curiosity of his account of the Faustian spring that it involves a bifurcation of the history of Christianity (II, 261). What provided Western culture with its new religion, he claims – and he is like Toynbee in regarding a youthful religion as indispensable to the rise of a culture – was the reform of the papacy in the tenth century and the appearance of a 'dynamic' doctrine of personal contrition and the Mother-of-God cult (II, 293; I, 267). The resulting 'Germanized' Christianity took over many of the outer trappings of its Magian predecessor; but, according to Spengler, it retained little of its 'inward form', and nothing of its 'world-feeling' (II, 237, 248).

Summer, in all cultures, sees the rise of towns, still integrated with the countryside, the growth of a more mannered aristocracy, and the appearance of the 'Third Estate' (II, 334). There are great individual artists now, like Polygnotus and Aeschylus, Michelangelo and Shakespeare (I, 282-3), and philosophy and science begin to develop in ways that promise future conflict with myth and religion – for example, the speculations of the nature philosophers of ancient Greece, or the probing inquiries of a Bacon or a Galileo. Intellect is still, however, basically supportive of the culture 'soul'. In the Apollinian world, this was the period of the early city-states, roughly the seventh and sixth centuries BC, and into the fifth. In the Faustian, it was the Renaissance and Reformation, and into the seventeenth century. The Dionysian movement in Greece 'corresponds' to the European Renaissance; the replacement of Doric by the more ornamented Ionic 'corresponds' to the passage of Gothic architecture into the Baroque; and what Pythagoras does for mathematics in the Apollinian culture, Descartes does, and at precisely the same stage, for the Faustian (I, 27, 205, 112). There are nevertheless some interesting differences in the way certain aspects of the two cultures developed. For example, the Faustian spirit soon outran the expressive possibilities of the plastic arts and found its outlet increasingly in oil painting and instrumental music. By contrast, in the Classical world, 'music was the art that failed' (I, 244-5).

With autumn comes a maturing of summer trends, and the first hints of a kind of cultural exhaustion. There is increased urban sophistication, the spread of commerce, and a move towards political centralization that eventually ruins the natural aristocracy. Intellect now poses a serious challenge to religion, and, in general, tradition is undermined by 'enlightenment' (not a laudatory term in Spengler's vocabulary). Art, science and philosophy reach new heights of creativity and power. But towards the end of the period, the townsmen make social revolution; and the generals, who are destined to supersede them, begin to make their appearance. In the Apollinian world this was the fifth and fourth centuries BC, with their Sophists, Socrates and 'definitive' philosophical systems, and that 'Maturity of Athens', of which the Acropolis was the perfect architectural expression. In the Faustian world it was the seventeenth and eighteenth centuries, culminating in the music of Mozart, the poetry of Goethe, and the philosophy of Kant. The French Revolution is the first breath of winter.

As winter sets in, creativity and style rapidly disappear, and culture hardens into what Spengler sometimes calls 'mere civilization'. The World City, or 'megalopolis', appears – Babylon, Thebes, Alexandria, Benares, Baghdad, Rome, London, Berlin, New York – with urban 'intelligence' replacing the 'soul' of the countryside (I, 32-3; II, 99). With the rise of a plutocracy, money dissolves personal relations, and gives rise to a rootless proletariat, 'a new sort of nomad, cohering unstably in fluid masses, the parasitical city-dweller' (I, 32, 35-6). Both the plutocracy and the proletariat, however, fall victim eventually to the military, as a period of almost continuous warfare begins – a period of 'contending Caesars', which can end only in the universal rule of one of them (II, 432).

Meanwhile, a vulgarized art loses its sense of form, degenerating into the merely esoteric or faddish (one could guess Spengler's reaction to electronic music or metal sculpture) (I, 35). Thought, too, becomes barren, as philosophy falls into skepticism, academic triviality or resignation (logical positivism or existentialism?) (I, 43, 45). What Spengler calls a 'second religiousness' also appears, as first the intelligentsia, then the masses, turn to cults, generally borrowed ones (like 'the Buddhism of the drawing room'), to fill the spiritual void, or retreat into mere piety without conviction (I, 424; II, 310). Thus a culture ends, as well as begins, in religion, although in religion of a very different kind.[15] The nearest thing to creativity in the winter period is science; but this is increasingly applied science: science devoting itself to problems of industry, bureaucracy, and, above all, to war. In the Apollinian world, winter begins with the adventures of Alexander the Great, and culminates in the rise to power of Julius Caesar. In the Faustian world, it is initiated by Napoleon, who, Spengler insists, is morphologically analogous not to Caesar, with whom he is so often compared, but to the earlier Alexander (I, 4, 38). Our own Caesar is still to come (II, 416). Spengler hopes he will be German (II, 109), although he seems to wonder, at one point, whether it may not be the United States that is destined to play the dreary role of Rome in our society (II, 99).

No matter how such details are resolved, Spengler's attempt to 'predetermine' history clearly issues in a depressing prognosis in our own case. We are doomed, he tells us, to a final drying up of the spirit. 'We are civilized, not Gothic or Rococo people; we have to reckon with the hard cold facts of a *late* life . . . Of great painting or great music there can no longer be, for Western people, any question. Their architectural possibilities have been exhausted these hundred years' (I, 40). Alone open to us are 'extensive possibilities': that is, feats of technology and administration appropriate to an age of Caesars — activities that will, at any rate, spread a culture to which we can no longer really contribute. Faustian youth should therefore be encouraged to devote itself 'to technics instead of lyrics, the sea instead of the paint brush, and politics instead of epistemology' (I, 41). The final message is thus to move with history, rather than to strain vainly against it. Spengler exhorts us to embrace our fate, rather than merely to suffer it — and, indeed, to do this with something akin to Roman pride.


## VI

So much for an elaboration of some salient features of Spengler's speculative vision of history. There are three critical questions I want to raise about it. First, I want to go back to Spengler's own description of the main thrust of his work, his claim that he has discovered a way of 'predetermining' history, to ask to what extent and in what way his theory is in fact predictive, and how his views on prediction relate to his conception of the nature of historical understanding. Second, I want to ask how good an historian he is — not in the sense of having done original research on documents and artefacts, since, as I mentioned earlier, he is not, in this sense, an historian at all — but simply in the sense of being able to produce a reasonable degree of empirical support for his conclusions, even at second hand. Third, I want to ask how consistent, and indeed in the end how intelligible, Spengler's system of ideas really is, taken even just as a system of ideas: that is, as what we might call a speculative 'hypothesis'. The latter two questions must sooner or later arise for *any* speculative philosophy of history. I might therefore preface what may sometimes seem a rather jaundiced account of how Spengler could respond to them, with the remark that the record of speculative philosophies is, in general, a rather poor one in this connection.


## VII

Spengler's defenders sometimes insist that it is a mistake to judge his work as if he were trying to construct some new kind of social science. What it offers is rather, they often tell us, an imaginative 'vision'[16] of the past, whose truth is 'the truth of poetry'. Indeed, Spengler sometimes talks this way himself. 'The wish to write history scientifically', he contends, 'involves a contradiction . . . Nature is to be handled scientifically, History poetically' (I, 96). But poetry is not predictive; and Spengler claims nothing if not to be able to predict. His book comes complete with fold-out tables on which the thousand-year life-spans of selected cultures are, seemingly, carefully worked out. There is also, of course, his uncompromising assessment of the prospects of the West, to which I have just called attention. Spengler has no second thoughts about the latter; he makes no *conditional* predictions; he is not telling us what will happen *unless* we do certain things. One does not find him, like Toynbee, wondering, at the end, whether God may perhaps grant us a 'reprieve' if we ask for it 'in a contrite spirit and with a broken heart'.[17]

There are nevertheless important limits to what Spengler claims to be able to predict; and perhaps also to his acceptance of the idea of historical determinism. For example, he is content to leave the origins of cultures a cosmic mystery: the rise of a new 'world-feeling' is, for him, something to be celebrated rather than to be understood (II, 33). All we can know, he says, is that, from time to time, 'a great soul awakens out of the proto-spirituality . . . of ever-childish humanity', and a new culture is born (I, 106). Its birth, furthermore, occurs suddenly: 'In one moment, the Romanesque style was there' (I, 201). Spengler allows, too, as I mentioned earlier, that, once born, a culture may deviate from the normal pattern of development, or at any rate fail to achieve adequate expressions of its basic orientation, due to pressures from its neighbours. It may also be swept away by external assault, or linger on as a mere civilization. None of these eventualities are historically determined in Spengler's special sense of following from the inner nature, or 'destiny', of the cultures concerned[18] (although, for all he shows to the contrary, they might, of course, be determined in some other way).

It should be noted, too, that even in the case of normal development, it is only the overall pattern of a culture that Spengler claims to be able to predict. What is determined, he says (using a characteristically figurative turn of phrase), is only the 'themes', not the 'modulations' (I, 145). The latter depend on the particular individuals involved. Thus it was Germany's destiny, Spengler tells us, to be united in the nineteenth century. But how it would be united depended on what Frederick William IV would do in 1848 and Bismarck in 1870 (I, 144–5). Evidently, 'destiny' is not seen as strictly determining the actions of individuals, but only as limiting them (II, 507)[19] — part of the rationale of Spengler's eventual call to political action.

At the level of what he sometimes calls mere 'incident', Spengler even finds a role for chance in history. Thus, of one fateful historical moment, from the standpoint of Faustian culture, at any rate, he observes: 'Chance decreed that the heavy attacks of the Huns should break themselves in vain upon the Chinese "Limes",' the result being that 'the Huns turned westward' (II, 41). Concerning another such moment, he speculates that, if Charles Martel had not been available to win the battle of Poitiers in AD 732, 'giant cities like Granada and Kairawan would have arisen on the Loire and the Rhine, [and] the Gothic feeling would have been forced to find expression in the long-stiffened forms of Mosque and Arabesque' (II, 192). When what is at issue is the possibility of pseudomorphosis — a notion which bulks larger and larger in *The Decline of the West* as one reads — Spengler is even prepared, at times, to say what *ought* to have happened but did not. Thus he declares that, at Actium, 'it should have been Antony who won' (II, 191), since this would have spared the Magian world 'the hard sheet of Roman Imperium'. Clearly, Spengler's 'modulations' swallow up a good deal of what is ordinarily thought of as the stuff of history.

The apparent looseness of the historical determinism to which Spengler seems actually to commit himself has sometimes provoked criticism. Collingwood, for example, complains that Spengler's so-called predictions are a fraud because what he has to say about the future is not specific. Thus we are told that by the end of the present century someone 'corresponding' to Caesar will appear in Faustian culture. But *who* will he be, Collingwood asks, and when *exactly* will he appear?[20] Doubtless Collingwood is reacting here like the good historian he is. For an historian, there are no more important questions than 'when?', 'where?', 'how?', and 'who?' — not even the question 'why?'[21] In the present context, however, this sort of criticism is surely a mistake. Predictions are made at various levels of specificity, even in the natural sciences; and no predictions are ever absolutely specific. In any case, Spengler does not just say that someone 'corresponding' to Caesar will appear. He says that a world conqueror will appear, and will set up a Faustian empire — something that we only missed by a hairbreadth, and only a little ahead of schedule, just a generation after he made the claim.

In fact, some of Spengler's predictions are quite specific enough to be arresting, and even disturbing. Erich Heller expresses what must surely be the response of many of his readers when he observes that 'the history of the West since 1917 looks like the work of children clumsily filling in with lurid colours a design drawn in outlines by Oswald Spengler.'[22] What is peculiar about Spengler's predictions is not so much their alleged looseness as two other features of them. First, they often seem less concerned with future events and states of affairs as such than with the *style*, and even the *value*, of what will occur in a given culture at a given time. In our own case, as we have seen, this takes the form of a denial that certain types of creativity are possible for us, given our cultural age. It is as if Spengler could at least rough out the critical notices of any of our attempts at music or poetry or philosophy before we even begin. The second peculiarity is that he takes no steps to support his predictive claims by any kind of detailed explanatory analysis. For example, he offers no account in terms of various kinds of causal factors that would help us see *why* things must go in the direction he declares to be inevitable.

With regard to the first of these peculiarities, some of Spengler's defenders would doubtless argue that it is precisely in the notion of historical inquiry as concerned with a cultural ageing process — this carrying with it the need to raise questions of style and value — that Spengler had something really important (and, at the time, at least, original) to say. Frye, for example, would maintain that, to a considerable degree, we are all Spenglerians now. The idea of belonging to a culture that is 'old', he says, is 'as much a part of our mental outlook today as the electron or the dinosaur'.[23] Certainly Spengler is one of the theorists who gave currency to this idea; there are eloquent passages in his book about 'the metaphysically-*exhausted* soil of the West', or the 'practical world-sentiment of *tired* megapolitans' (indeed, when encountered by certain German chieftains, Magian civilization is said to have been '*pale* and tired') (I, 5, 356; II, 87 (my italics)). I confess, however, that I find this idea of cultural ageing a very puzzling one. For although Spengler sometimes talks as if it is the individuals who live in late periods of a culture whom he believes to be afflicted by a kind of weariness of spirit, it seems clear that his real thesis is that the culture itself suffers the ageing process — this raising the whole problem of what (in chapter III) was called ontological individualism. For example, when he represents cultural ageing as the progressive exhaustion of expressive possibilities in a given style, he doesn't seem to want to mean anything as straightforward as a progressive closing-off of such possibilities simply because they have been exploited already — there being no merit in doing the same thing twice. The latter is, perhaps, the way in which a methodological individualist, like Watkins, would try to interpret the doctrine. But it is doubtful that any such 'reductive' approach would be mysterious enough for Spengler. In section IX I shall consider a more specific problem that arises out of the way he actually employs the notion of 'cultural age'.

With regard to the second peculiarity of Spengler's claims to be able to predict, it should be noted that his rejection of causal analysis is, in fact, just an extreme form of a notion — Hughes calls it a 'romantic' one[24] — that has been very much alive in the philosophy of history of the last hundred years, and which we found in a more muted (and I think more acceptable) form in Collingwood. This is the notion that, by its very nature, causal investigation carves up the living in the process of trying to understand it, and in consequence, fails to understand it for what it is, namely living (I, 95).[25] Spengler has what can only be called a great loathing for the idea of causation (II, 31). For him, it falls on the wrong side of a whole series of related contrasts: instinct versus intellect, form versus law, becoming versus become, organism versus mechanism, country versus town, blood versus money, time versus space, culture versus civilization, history versus nature — and, eventually, life versus death. So great was his aversion to what he regarded as the overly intellectual procedure of breaking up living processes into causes and effects that he said that the first task of any would-be historian of the new Spenglerian age would be to learn *how not to think* — by which he apparently means *how to not think* (I, 151, 119). So stated, it is hard to take his position entirely seriously.

Yet the underlying uneasiness about causal analysis is not peculiar to Spengler. It is a pity, therefore, that, unlike most philosophers who might be referred to as 'idealist', and with whom, in view of his making history an affair of 'spirit' he would seem to have some affinity, he offered no alternative account of how the large-scale historical movements that he saw as especially important are to be related to what might, in some more detailed and analytical way explain them. If he had tried to deal with this problem, instead of using his organic analogy as, in effect, a theoretical barrier against further questioning, he would have had to begin by distinguishing two issues which, in his attacks on causal thinking, he constantly runs together.

The first is whether history should be explained *mechanistically*. In giving a negative answer, Spengler often talks as if he thinks the causal relation is necessarily mechanical in a literal sense: something like a collision of billiard-balls (I, 93).[26] Clearly, if he excluded only judgments of this kind from history, he would exclude very little. At other times, what he seems to have chiefly in mind is explaining in terms of physical factors;[27] at still others, in terms of factors which are rigorously quantifiable (I, 100). But that would still leave a host of putative explanations, naturally framed in causal terms, for the rejection of which he would need quite different reasons — in fact, most of the explanations citing social conditions or the beliefs and intentions of individuals that historians normally give. At still other points, what he means by causal explanation seems more to resemble Collingwood's notion of understanding from the 'outside': that is, bringing what is to be explained under natural laws ('Nature', by contrast with 'History', Spengler declares, is 'the sum of the law-imposed necessities' (I, 95)). Unfortunately, unlike Collingwood, he never seriously addresses the problem of what, with reference to this criterion, a *non*-causal explanation would be like; he never asks, for example, whether there are any important differences between citing causes and citing reasons, although there are hints of explanatory reasons in some of his own historical diagnoses, if only at the level of what he calls 'mere incident' (see his explanation of Napoleon's incorporation of Germany and Spain, I, 150). What he tends to contrast with explanation by law is understanding intuitively, which is not another *kind* of explanation, but an alleged method for achieving it. His failure, in the end, to provide any positive account of historical understanding, by contrast with the recognition of 'law-imposed necessities', leads critics like Collingwood to accuse him of being a surreptitious positivist, for all his protestations to the contrary.[28] There is no provision in his approach to history, Collingwood justly complains, for the perception of human life as a mental achievement, and hence as a re-thinkable rational process.

The other question is whether history should be explained *reductively*. I say 'reductively' rather than 'individualistically' because Spengler opposes accounting for large-scale processes, not only in terms of the actions of individuals (as advocated, for example, by Watkins) but also in terms of parts or aspects of such processes. In attacking what he calls the 'rationalist' school of history, he even denies that it is ever 'permissible to fix upon one, any one, group of social, religious, physiological or ethical facts as the "cause" of another' (I, 155). For Spengler, good historical explanation always proceeds by reference to the whole; and one of the things he means, when he talks of causal explanation derogatorily, is any kind that proceeds in other directions. Indicative of the holistic kind of explanation of which Spengler himself approves, are his relating the 'vehemence' of the Arab onslaught on Europe and North Africa in the seventh and eighth centuries to the long frustration of the Magian spirit, deprived as it had been of 'lands that had inwardly belonged to it for centuries past' (I, 213); and his accounting for the internecine struggles of the Greeks by reference to their view of the world as composed of discrete and limited entities, 'the need of bodily separation' between the various 'point-patriae' therefore taking 'the form of hatreds far more intense than any hatred that there was of the Barbarian' (I, 335). Whether such explanations are actually irreducible — for example, to what anonymous Arabs and Greeks believed and felt — will, of course, depend on the kind of considerations discussed in chapter III. Spengler makes a less disputable claim when he protests that discerning 'the operations of cause and effect' will not 'give unity to the story of development' (I, 281): that is, it will not provide what was earlier called 'synthetic' explanation. That is true; but it is hardly a good reason for proscribing causal (in the sense of 'analytic') explanation altogether.


## VIII

My second large question is how well Spengler's theory is supported empirically. Spengler has been accused by many critics of playing fast and loose with historical facts to a degree that is extreme even for a speculative philosopher of history. In trying to decide whether such criticism is justified, it is important to remember again that his analysis of cultures has two parts or aspects. What comes out of it, finally, is the account of the normal pattern of cultural development (it is hard not to call this a 'law', in spite of Spengler's own distaste for this terminology, and in spite of the qualifications now seen to apply to it). But antecedent to this is the identification of particular cultures, and of the historical circumstances which, in each case, counted as passing through the various stages of the ageing process. The burden of factual justification is somewhat different for the two parts of the theory, so I shall consider them in turn.

Whatever Spengler himself would have said about it, his four-phase 'law' seems to be based, in the end, on inductive reasoning of the simplest kind. What is found true of particular cases examined is taken to be true for all members of the class of things under study. Spengler himself sometimes talks as if he might not accept this account of what he is doing. For example, he states explicitly in the preface to the second edition of his first volume that his 'idea' (and one assumes that he means this to include his major claims) has only to be 'understood' to be seen to be 'irrefutable'. And he often talks of the 'inherent necessities' of the cultural developments he has in view as if he directly perceived the latter,[29] and not just the nature of the various culture 'souls', by means of his vaunted 'physiognomic tact' (I, 400, 418). But if calling attention to such directly intuitable necessities is the burden of what he has to say, it is difficult to see the point of his insisting that historians engage in *comparative* morphology. Unless the comparison of different cultural developments is to be treated as an implicit argument of some kind, most of Spengler's book becomes a gross irrelevancy. One can still agree with critics such as A.L. Kroeber that Spengler's inquiry is more comparative in intent than in execution.[30] What matters for present purposes is the intent.

If Spengler's inquiry is genuinely comparative, however, its empirical weakness is very plain. He has only nine specimens of what he wants to generalize about. Of these, several are admitted to have developed abnormally; and only three (one might even say two) are known at all well. If Spengler could have provided some reasons, other than his comparative tables, for expecting that cultures as such would be subject to the four-stage law — if, for example, he had (as I suggested above) offered some kind of explanation of the pattern's holding even in the cases examined, this throwing light, perhaps, on the nature of the ageing process — he would have been on firmer ground. But his exclusion of all explanatory analysis puts him out of reach of this kind of support. In consequence, his claim to have found a generally recurring pattern of cultural development is very weak. In this regard, Toynbee is in an incomparably better position, working with a group of cultural specimens numbering, in the beginning, twenty-one, and increasing to over thirty as his study progressed.

But even if nothing deserving of the name of a law of cultural development could be derived from comparing the specimens Spengler examines, his identification of particular cultures, and the stages that each *in fact* went through, would still be of great interest. It is thus worth asking independently what degree of factual support he can muster for the claims he wishes to make at this logically prior level of inquiry. It will be remembered that his identification of particular cultures is based on alleged perceptions of deep stylistic differences between ways of feeling and behaving observed in a broad survey of human history. We need to ask how plausible these alleged perceptions really are.

Almost anyone will surely find some of them both acceptable and illuminating. It is hard not to be moved, for example, by the observation that 'the chimes of countless clock towers that echo day and night over West Europe' constitute 'the most wonderful expression' of the Faustian 'world-feeling' (I, 14). And almost anyone can see that flying buttresses symbolize a feeling of living in infinite space better than Greek pediments do. However, the going soon gets tougher. Perhaps, with an effort, most of us can catch a glimpse of the way a Doric column symbolizes 'the pure present' (I, 9), or descry the 'deep uniformities' said by Spengler to hold between historical movements like Classical stoicism and Western socialism (I, 357-9), or Mohammedanism and English Puritanism (II, 303). But we may surely be excused a certain feeling of dizziness on finding contrapuntal music compared with credit economics, the differential calculus with dynastic politics, and Rembrandt's deep browns with Beethoven's music for strings (I, 7, 252). Nor is it at all easy to see that bluish-green is, by its very nature, and not simply through custom or historical accident, a Catholic colour, while brown is a Protestant one (I, 247).

What has most disturbed Spengler's critics, however, is not the boldness, or even the occasional incomprehensibility of his judgments. It is that, besides being intrinsically dubitable, they have often seemed too obviously responsive to the needs of his theory as a whole to be easily accepted as independent cultural appraisals. Thus, since Spinoza had what Spengler is forced to regard as some very non-Faustian views on substance, and was conveniently a Jew, he is classified as a 'belated representative of the Magian' (I, 307; II, 321).[31] Since the empire of Charlemagne occurred too early to be included in the thousand year life-span of Western culture, and clearly wasn't Magian, it is considered 'non-historical': at most, a kind of Faustian stirring in the womb (II, 362). The Greeks, being necessarily afflicted by Classical man's 'metaphysical shyness' of distance, are described as essentially stay-at-homes, in spite of their having colonized the Mediterranean: for Spengler, apparently, they didn't go far enough — failing, for example, to sail on to the south coast of Africa, as some of their Carthaginian and Egyptian predecessors had done, or even to penetrate to the interior where they did land (I, 333–4). Still more surprising, the Romans, necessarily lacking the expansive Faustian 'will', did not really conquer the world (I, 36, 310 n. 1): they merely 'took possession of a booty open to anyone' (one is reminded of one of Taylor's arguments about Hitler). How many, not already bemused by Spengler's system, would be prepared to concur in such judgments? Surely Huizinga was not far wrong in declaring it all to be 'rather reminiscent of the straining of evidence to harmonize the Old and the New Testaments in Christian apologetics'.[32]

Some critics have charged Spengler with actually distorting the facts, or at any rate suppressing some of them, in the service of his theory. Thus Frye protests that, in characterizing the Roman period of Classical history as uncreative, Spengler ignores completely the Roman poets, Lucretius, Virgil, Ovid, Horace and Catullus.[33] And Collingwood complains that, in representing the Greeks as polytheists, as their 'world-feeling' supposedly requires, he ignores the monotheism of the Greek philosophers — although showing himself willing enough to cite the latter when they behave in appropriately Apollinian ways.[34] Collingwood points out, too, that Spengler's view of Classical man as expressing his commitment to the here-and-now by burning rather than burying the dead has to face such apparently contrary evidence as the miles of tombs along the Appian Way at Rome. In fact, in the latter case at least, Spengler cannot be accused of *suppressing* the facts, since he actually mentions the tombs in question (I, 34); and he might perhaps contend that, being late phenomena, they are uncharacteristic. His notion of pseudomorphosis gives him further room for manoeuvre — for example, allowing him to explain away the dome on the Roman Pantheon as an irruption of the Magian into the Classical world: 'the earliest of all Mosques' (I, 72). Before making any final judgment on the empirical worth of Spengler's identification of cultures, it would be necessary to review systematically what he says about such examples. Even the ones cited, however, surely raise doubts about the fundamental judgments — the aesthetic 'facts' — upon which the whole Spenglerian view of history ultimately rests.

I should perhaps add that, in thus questioning the empirical adequacy of Spengler's system, I am not implicitly accepting two arguments which are commonly levelled against him in this connection. The first is that his account of world history is highly *selective*. Since, as was noted in chapter II in discussing Beard, all history is necessarily selective, this can hardly, in itself, be considered a fault. For just as we properly demand of a workaday historian an interpretive hypothesis which can be supported by the citation of relevant, and therefore selected, facts, so we should of a speculative philosopher of history. What one suspects in Spengler's case is that, although he cites plenty of facts that (to the extent they can be understood) seem relevant enough, he does not look very hard for facts which, if he found them, would show his hypothesis to be unsound. His method (and Toynbee's, unfortunately, resembles it in this respect) is very much that of empirical *exemplification*: indeed, he tells us so himself (I, xiv). What is needed, however, is a procedure of empirical *testing*; and this would require a clearer conception of what the interpretive hypothesis rules out than Spengler generally seems to provide. If the Roman poets or the Greek philosophers would not be counted as tending to falsify his hypothesis, we need a clearer view of what would. Not that the ways Spengler sometimes does deal with apparently contrary evidence are always unacceptable: for example, through appeal to notions of pseudomorphosis, or the survival of cultural residues, or the existence of cultures in embryo. For these (although they need to be made more precise) do not involve the rejection of contrary facts *ad hoc*; they represent a refinement of the hypothesis itself. However, not all the facts that seem to offer difficulties for Spengler fall easily into such categories.

The other argument is that Spengler doesn't proceed empirically at all, and doesn't intend to do so; his theory, it is sometimes said, is offered to us *a priori*. Now in one very important sense this is clearly untrue. For even if Spengler believes that a certain kind of insight is needed to discern the facts he claims to discern, he reaches his conclusions by putting that insight to work in a study of the actual course of events; and he invites us to do the same. There is no question, for example, of his deriving his doctrines from first principles, by pure reason, or by means of any kind of intuition without reference to empirical facts. Perhaps what lies behind the charge of *a priorism*, then, is simply the realization that one cannot bring Spenglerian interpretive categories to bear on history without making value-judgments, especially aesthetic ones. But since, as was argued in chapter II, one cannot do history at all without making such judgments, there would seem to be no objection in principle to Spengler's procedure in this connection either. What needs to be challenged is not the legitimacy of his making aesthetic judgments, but some of the judgments, aesthetic and otherwise, that he actually makes.

Spengler is sometimes accused of *a priorism* in still a further, but also dubious, sense. Hughes, for example, complains that 'when his knowledge proves insufficient, he is driven to desperate expedients': while writing of 'an obscure epoch of Chinese history', for example, he states that 'things *must* have happened in a certain fashion'.[35] That Spengler occasionally does this sort of thing is quite true (II, 285). Once again, however, it is far from clear than he can be denied such procedures, on principle, in the name of good historical method. Even Collingwood, the author of perhaps the most severe critique of Spengler in English, found room in his own account of history in *The Idea of History* for a certain amount of what he called 'interpolation'. If an historian knows that Caesar was at one time in Gaul and at another time in Rome, he says, he may with a perfectly good conscience interpolate a journey he must have taken — presumably on the authority of our general knowledge of such matters.[36] In a sense, this could be called *'a priori'* history; but only in the sense of asserting that for which one lacks direct evidence, not that for which one has no empirical justification at all. What is wrong in Spengler's case is not that he occasionally does much the same thing, but that he does it on the authority of a general account of the historical process which itself lacks sufficient empirical justification.

## IX

The third question I said I wanted to consider — that of the degree of coherence achieved by the Spenglerian system of ideas — is quite as important for the appraisal of his overall view of history as is the question of the soundness of his judgments of the 'aesthetic facts'. For one can hardly even discuss the degree of empirical support enjoyed by a theory unless the theory formulates a coherent hypothesis. And critics have, in fact, found a number of dimensions of difficulty in the way Spengler formulates his 'hypothesis'. I shall consider two of these which seem of particular interest and importance. The first arises out of what he has to say about a lack of real connection, and even of real communication, between the cultures he distinguishes. The second derives from the way he relates differences of cultural style and differences of cultural age, in drawing upon the sorts of judgments I have just been considering.

It is vital for Spengler's predictive goals, and also for his general attack on linear interpretations of history, that cultures be what might be called *self*-determining systems. They must be 'pre-programmed' as it were: not open to major modification by what impinges on them from without. In particular, Spengler cannot allow that any essential change can occur in what he takes to be the most important fact about a culture, namely its style. This means that he cannot allow that members of one culture can ever adopt or otherwise absorb anything of significance in this respect from another. He protects himself against the latter possibility by maintaining, not only that cultures never learn from one another, but also that they never really understand each other (what one cannot understand one cannot learn, and what one cannot learn one cannot be influenced by). Spengler was so committed to this latter thesis that he was willing to apply it even to such an apparently unlikely case as mathematics. In a famous and formidable chapter, which, with typical disregard for the comfort of his readers he placed at the beginning of his book, he argued that Classical, Magian and Faustian man, appearances to the contrary, have entirely different conceptions of number. Thus, when modern Europeans, for example, 'learn' Euclidean geometry, although they may go through the same motions, they simply do not mean by them what the Greeks did; they take over Greek forms but impart their own meanings to them. For Classical man, what mathematics was all about is magnitude; for Faustian man, what it is about is function (I, 75). The whole history of Western mathematics, according to Spengler, has, in fact, been 'a long, secret and finally victorious battle against the notion of magnitude' (I, 76). Other examples of one culture failing to learn from another what it really had to teach are Indian and Chinese Buddhists continuing to be 'two different souls, each going its own way' (I, 57), Calvin's converting Augustine's dualistic and substantialistic notion of grace into one of dynamic will (II, 59), and Shakespeare's making a Faustian hero out of Julius Caesar (I, 146).

Now even ordinary experience gives a certain measure of support to such a notion of cultures being radically cut off from each other. Westerners, for example, have long wondered whether they would ever have a real conversation with the Chinese (and are not sure they have had one yet). We may hope that misunderstandings of other cultures, although deep, are only temporary; but this hope is sometimes hard to maintain in practice. However, when Spengler asserts what we may call his 'cultural isolation' thesis,[37] he isn't just acknowledging that it is very hard *in practice* for one culture to understand another. He is claiming that it is impossible in principle: and this raises a characteristic difficulty. For it seems to conflict, among other things, with his own implicit claim, in writing *The Decline of the West*, to have understood all alien cultures. His own comparative morphology surely *presupposes* the possibility of such understanding. Otherwise, all he could have thought he was elaborating is a Faustian

121

*mis*understanding of World History — or, if that is too strong, then, at any rate, an account of it from a strictly Faustian point of view, which sounds very like what he began by criticizing the 'Ptolemaic' historians for doing.

In fact, there are hints that Spengler might not have entirely rejected something like the latter idea. Thus he declares: 'my own philosophy is able to express and reflect *only* the Western (as distinct from the Classical, Indian or other) soul' (I, 46); and he sometimes represents the writing of universal history as itself a distinctively Faustian activity — a kind of outreaching intellectual imperialism, ranging over the whole of past time in a manner quite foreign to cultures lacking the Western 'historical feeling' (II, 394). In this mood, his claim for his own work seems to be that it constitutes the last, best creation of the philosophy of the West (I, 159). However, the latter claim has difficulties of its own; for early winter is not the time, according to Spengler's own charts, for the appearance of a culture's culminating philosophical system (I, 98) — that particular accolade having, in any case, already been bestowed upon the philosophy of Kant (I, 365). Late autumn and early winter are the periods when nature study, and more generally, scientific thinking, are alone supposed to be able to flourish; and Spengler has made it very clear that he regards scientific and historical thinking as polar opposites. Unkind critics might be tempted, at this point, to suggest that his system turns out here to be sounder than he knew — his own attempt to see history in terms of normal patterns of cultural development being, in fact, an attempt to study history scientifically, just as those who accuse him of positivism have maintained.

However, Spengler does not always try to meet the original difficulty by relativizing his claims to a Faustian point of view. A solution which he seems often to prefer is to hold that, from time to time, there appear great intuitive geniuses (like himself) who can rise above the relativity of ordinary historical understanding and take 'a high, time-free perspective' (I, 34) — a claim reminiscent of that of Marx to have escaped the conditioning of his bourgeois background in writing *his* account of history. But if Spengler takes this second way out — and if we can assume, dubiously, that it makes sense to try to eliminate points of view altogether — a different problem arises. For it seems reasonable to ask: Who was he writing for? What about the 100,000 copies? Surely he didn't think that his study of history, being transcultural in nature, could not be grasped by those Faustian fellow-countrymen to whom it was especially addressed. However, if he allows that his readers can understand his account of other cultures, and continues to hold that the only thing preventing cultural borrowing is a failure to understand, then it isn't at all clear why one culture could not borrow from another. And if this is possible at all, it isn't clear either how Spengler can set theoretical limits to how much borrowing can go on, and what its consequences could be. This problem is absolutely crucial for him. For, as I have emphasized, the special kind of predictability he sees in history depends entirely upon the inexorability of the cultural ageing process; and the latter apparently depends upon people being locked into their cultures.

Serious difficulties also arise out of the way in which Spengler commonly distinguishes between differences of cultural style and differences of cultural age, when discussing the significance of the various expressive phenomena he considers.[38] Let me say again just what these distinctions involve. The contrast between, for example, a Doric column and a Gothic spire would be a contrast of cultural style: the one is Apollinian, the other Faustian; the one expresses the idea of infinite space, the other of local place. On the other hand, the contrast between a Bach fugue and contemporary rock music would be a contrast of cultural age: both are Faustian, but the one is young and the other old. Some of Spengler's most striking reinterpretations of historical personages, events and conditions exploit his judgments of how they exemplify both of these contrasts at once (as, of course, any significant cultural phenomenon would necessarily do). For example, Buddha is an Indian religious figure who, as the founder of a world religion, is often compared with Christ. But, according to Spengler, Buddha belongs to the Indian winter, and expresses the resignation appropriate to that phase of its culture. By contrast, Christ is a figure of the Magian spring, and expresses a new 'world-feeling' in a simple, fresh, youthful form (I, 361). Thus the 'physiognomic tact' of the Spenglerian historian must play two different roles: it must determine cultural style, but it must also recognize cultural age. It is important to see that judgments of age, as much as judgments of style, are *aesthetic* judgments. Being a spring or winter phenomenon is not just a matter of chronology: it is a matter of expressing the basic style of a culture in appropriately different ways.[39] The analogy is with youth and senility in the human being. Being senile is not just being chronologically old; it is 'acting old'; and we can recognize a man to be senile regardless of his chronological age.

The problem is that when Spengler tries to explain why he classifies a given phenomenon as he does with regard to style and with regard to age, we sometimes find him supporting these quite different judgments by reference to the same sorts of considerations. Thus he regards it as typically Faustian to reach out into space and occupy it, and thus be imperialistic. And this characteristic of the Faustian spirit is traced back to its most splendid period, showing itself, for example, in the political ambitions of the Saxon, Franconian and Hauenstaufen emperors, and the corresponding religious ones of popes Gregory VII and Innocent III (I, 198). But Spengler also sees imperialism as a sign of old age in all cultures, a 'typical symbol of . . . passing away' (I, 36): even the static Greek culture and the meandering Chinese one had their world empires. To take another example: the Buddhist ideal of 'Nirvana' is 'thoroughly Indian, and traceable even from Vedic times' (I, 347). But an attitude of resignation (or of 'nihilism', Buddha being also a nihilist, according to Spengler), is characteristic of every culture at the stage of its 'second religiousness' (II, 311). To say the least, such an overlap of criteria imports a certain arbitrariness into the conclusions eventually drawn.

The difficulty is compounded when what Spengler has to say about age differences is taken together with his cultural isolation thesis. At more than one point, he tells us that people cannot really understand what is culturally 'out of phase' with them. Thus, according to him, although *we* can understand the revolution of Tiberius Gracchus in the late autumn of the Roman world, since we are roughly at the same stage in our own cultural development, the Roman writer, Tacitus, living deep in the Roman winter, could not understand its significance at all (II, 47). Neither, says Spengler, will our descendants understand it in 2200; and neither did our ancestors in 1700 (II, 50). For similar reasons, the painting of Rembrandt and the music of Mozart will one day cease to exist, even for Faustians (I, 168). If we put the two denials together, we are left in the following impasse. If we can understand neither what is out of phase with us, nor what is out of style with us, then apparently we can understand only ourselves. A philosophy of history that reaches a conclusion like that surely ought to retrace some of its steps.

# Notes

---

## Introduction

1 This term was given currency by W.H. Walsh's *An Introduction to Philosophy of History*, London, Hutchinson, 1951.

2 Penguin Books, 1964.

3 London, Allen Lane, 1970, pp. 113–14.

4 London, Allen Lane, 1972, pp. 7, 15.

5 Besides the books mentioned above, see also Elton's *The Practice of History*, London, Collins, 1969, and Hexter's *Doing History*, Indiana University Press, 1971.

6 See, for example, the spirited attack on the idea that philosophers of history need be 'useful' to historians in R.F. Atkinson, *Knowledge and Explanation in History*, Cornell University Press, 1978, p. 8.

7 The standards that Elton, in particular, seems ready to apply in such matters are enough to give a philosopher pause. An analysis offered by Alan Donagan, for example, is said to 'come to grief' because, by discussing the thesis of Trevor-Roper regarding a rising and falling gentry in seventeenth century England, it showed 'a readiness to treat as useful cases of historical explanation instances which historical research has had little difficulty in discarding' (p. 115). Patrick Gardiner is similarly scolded for having selected examples from G.M. Trevelyan's *English Social History*, which is written off as a 'repository of bogus explanations (facile and often meaningless generalizations plus artificial discoveries of "influence")' (p. 118).

8 Tr. C.F. Atkinson, London, Allen & Unwin, 1926, 1928; originally published in German in 1918 and 1922 (first volume revised in 1923).

9   A comparable discussion of Toynbee's view of history is to be found
    in my *Philosophy of History,* Englewood Cliffs, N.J., Prentice-Hall,
    1964, ch. 7.

## Chapter I   Collingwood and Actions in History

1   Clarendon Press, 1946. Page numbers in brackets in the text above
    refer to this work.
2   Clarendon Press, 1962. See also especially L.O. Mink, *Mind, History
    and Dialectic,* Indiana University Press, 1969, and Lionel Rubinoff,
    *Collingwood and the Reform of Metaphysics,* University of Toronto
    Press, 1970.
3   I discuss the first of these criticisms in 'Collingwood's Historical
    Individualism', forthcoming in the *Canadian Journal of Philosophy,*
    and others in a forthcoming book on Collingwood's philosophy of
    history. See also L.O. Mink, 'Collingwood's Historicism: A Dialectic
    of Process', in M. Krausz, ed., *Critical Essays in the Philosophy of
    R.G. Collingwood,* Clarendon Press, 1972, pp. 154-78.
4   The quoted passages are from pp. 213-16.
5   'The "Objects" of Historical Knowledge', *Philosophy,* 27, 1952,
    p. 213.
6   On this and what immediately follows see also my 'R.G. Collingwood
    and the Acquaintance Theory of Knowledge', *Revue internationale
    de philosophie,* 42: 4, 1957, pp. 420-32.
7   Donagan, *The Later Philosophy of R.G. Collingwood,* p. 200.
8   *An Introduction to Philosophy of History* (London, Hutchinson,
    1967, 3rd edn), p. 71. His subsequently modified this interpretation.
9   Op. cit., p. 201. See also his 'Explanation in History', in P. Gardiner,
    ed., *Theories of History,* Chicago, Free Press, 1959, p. 432.
10  Op. cit., p. 201.
11  Op. cit., p. 189.
12  The pros and cons of this contentious issue are nowhere dealt with
    directly in the present book. For a good overview of the problem
    see R.H. Weingartner, 'Historical Explanation', in Paul Edwards,
    ed., *Encyclopedia of Philosophy,* New York, Free Press, 1967, vol.
    4, pp. 7-12. For a sophisticated defence of an anti-Collingwoodian
    position, see M.G. White, *Foundations of Historical Knowledge,*
    New York, Harper & Row, 1965, chs 2-3.
13  See also *An Autobiography,* Oxford University Press, 1939, p. 128,
    n. 1.
14  'A Pluralist Approach to the Philosophy of History', in E. Streisler
    *et al., Roads to Freedom: Essays in Honour of F.A. Hayek,* London,
    Routledge & Kegan Paul, 1969, pp. 196 ff.
15  Op. cit., pp. 198-9.

16 *The Nature of Historical Explanation,* Oxford University Press, 1952, p. 30. See also his 'Historical Understanding: the Empiricist Tradition', in B.A. Williams and A. Montefiori, eds, *British Analytic Philosophy,* London, Routledge & Kegan Paul, 1966, p. 274.

17 *Philosophy and the Historical Understanding,* New York, Schocken, 1964, p. 18.

18 *Historians' Fallacies,* London, Routledge & Kegan Paul, 1971, p. 199.

19 *Political History,* London, Allen Lane, 1970, p. 133.

20 *A Study of History,* vol. IX, Oxford University Press, 1954, pp. 733–4. Toynbee takes Collingwood's requirement of re-experiencing the past to imply that the historian of Tamerlane should run amok in the streets.

21 This is approximately the position of C.G. Hempel in 'The Function of General Laws in History', in P. Gardiner, ed., *Theories of History,* New York, Free Press, 1959, p. 353.

22 *An Autobiography,* p. 128.

23 *Between Philosophy and History,* Princeton University Press, 1970, p. 144.

24 *What is History?,* New York, Vintage, 1967, p. 79.

25 *An Autobiography,* p. 152.

26 Ibid., p. 112.

27 Not, at any rate, in *The Idea of History,* apart from such passages as p. 132, where it is implied that the historian must 'judge' the facts.

## Chapter II   Beard and the Search for the Past

1 The first in 39: 2, 1934, pp. 219-31; the second in 41: 1, 1935, pp. 74-87. The first is reprinted in H. Meyerhoff, ed., *The Philosophy of History in Our Time,* Garden City, N.Y., Doubleday Anchor, 1959, pp. 140-51, and the second in F. Stern, ed., *The Varieties of History,* New York, Meridian, 1956, pp. 315-28. Page numbers in brackets in the text above prefaced 'WH' and 'ND' refer respectively to these sources. The second article is also included in R. Nash, ed., *Ideas of History,* vol. 2, New York, Dutton, 1969, under the title, 'The Case for Historical Relativism'.

2 Beard does not himself talk of 'objectivist' theory; but he does ask about 'the possibility of finding and stating the objective truth of history'; and again, whether we can 'grasp history objectively' ('ND' 317).

3 On this see A.C. Danto, *Analytical Philosophy of History,* Cambridge University Press, 1965, pp. 71 ff.

4 As in chapter I, section III, an acquaintance theory of knowledge

for history thus again comes under fire, but for a different reason.

5 See Danto, op. cit., ch. VIII.

6 For a way in which value-judgment may enter into causal judgment itself, when it goes beyond the mere discerning of necessary and sufficient conditions, see chapter IV below.

7 For a consideration of other kinds see also my 'On Importance in History', in H.E. Kiefer and M.K. Munitz, eds, *Mind, Science, and History,* State University of New York Press, 1970, pp. 251-69.

8 M.G. White entertains this possibility in 'Can History be Objective?', in Meyerhoff, op. cit., p. 195. This whole article offers a good critique of Beard's position.

9 What Beard actually calls 'transcendent' in stating his third argument is the structural hypothesis; but the above seems to catch at least part of what he means.

10 Some of the difficulties of doing history at that level are displayed in chapter V.

11 Cf. Collingwood's 'inside–outside' analysis of human action, chapter I, section II above.

12 The next two paragraphs retract part of the position I took (against Strauss and Winch) on the possibility of objectivity in historical description in *The Philosophy of History,* pp. 26-7.

13 This example was suggested to me by Mr Walter Sims.

14 For a consideration of the way aesthetic judgments may be constitutive of historical facts, see chapter V, section IV.

## Chapter III   Watkins and the Historical Individual

1 See, for example, E.H. Carr, *What is History?,* New York, Vintage, 1967, ch. 2; or G. Leff, *History and Social Theory,* University of Alabama Press, 1969, pp. 168ff.

2 See, for example, 'Ideal Types and Historical Explanation', in H. Feigl and M. Brodbeck, eds, *Readings in the Philosophy of Science,* New York, Appleton-Century-Crofts, 1953, pp. 723-43; 'Historical Explanation in the Social Sciences', in P. Gardiner, ed., *Theories of History,* New York, Free Press, 1959, pp. 503-15; 'Methodological Individualism: a Reply', *Philosophy of Science,* 22: 1, 1955, pp. 58-62; and 'The Alleged Inadequacy of Methodological Individualism', *Journal of Philosophy,* 55, 1958, pp. 390-5. Page numbers in brackets prefaced 'IT', 'HE', 'R' and 'AI' in the text above refer respectively to these sources. All of them, as well as some other writings cited below, are included in John O'Neill's excellent anthology, *Modes of Individualism and Collectivism,* London, Heinemann, 1973.

3 This use of 'intelligible' is not Watkins', but Ernest Gellner's in a

critique of Watkins's claims, but it seems to catch his sense. See Gellner's 'Holism versus Individualism in History and Sociology', in P. Gardiner, ed., *Theories of History*, pp. 492-3.

4 This remains true even if, as is commonly argued, what is distinctively human could not have come about except in a social context.

5 'Societal Facts', in P. Gardiner, ed., *Theories of History*, p. 486.

6 See *The Rules of Sociological Method*, tr. S.A. Solovay and J.H. Mueller, New York, Free Press, 1938, p. 102. Watkins singles out Durkheim for criticism in 'The Principle of Methodological Individualism', *British Journal for the Philosophy of Science*, 3: 10, 1952, p. 186.

7 For discussion of the problem raised by the existence of such properties see May Brodbeck, 'Methodological Individualisms: Definition and Reduction', in W.H. Dray, ed., *Philosophical Analysis and History*, New York, Harper & Row, 1966, pp. 297-329; and L.J. Goldstein, 'The Two Theses of Methodological Individualism', *British Journal for the Philosophy of Science*, 9: 33, 1956, pp. 1-11.

8 This issue comes up again in a different form in section VII.

9 See, for example, chapter IV, section IV: the whole of this chapter discusses possible criteria for the selection of causes.

10 The view attributed to Collingwood towards the end of chapter I, section IV.

11 See H.L.A. Hart and A.M. Honoré, *Causation in the Law*, Clarendon Press, 1959, p. 40.

12 This point has been emphasized also by Alan Donagan in 'Explanation in History', in P. Gardiner, ed., *Theories of History*, pp. 428-43, and M.G. White in *Foundations of Historical Knowledge*, New York, Harper & Row, 1965, pp. 47ff.

13 The best statement of this admittedly controversial interpretation of Collingwood is to be found in Alan Donagan, *The Later Philosophy of R.G. Collingwood*, Clarendon Press, 1962, pp. 230ff.

14 On this see also Collingwood, *The Idea of History*, Clarendon Press, 1946, p. 199.

15 Op. cit., pp. 15ff.

16 The example is Anthony Quinton's, in 'Social Objects', *Proceedings of the Aristotelian Society*, 76, 1975-6, p. 9.

17 'The Function of General Laws in History', in H. Feigl and W. Sellars, eds, *Readings in Philosophical Analysis*, New York, Appleton-Century-Crofts, 1949, p. 467. Cf. chapter I, note 21 above.

18 Mandelbaum's way of stating his position, in 'Societal Facts', p. 486.

19 This should not be taken as an endorsement of the so-called 'constructionist' theory of history as expounded, for example, by L.J. Goldstein in 'History and the Primacy of Knowing', *History and Theory*, 16: 4, 1977, pp. 29-52, which distinguishes sharply between the 'real' and the 'historical' pasts.

20 Discussion of this sort of explanation can be found in L.O. Mink, 'The Autonomy of Historical Understanding', in W.H. Dray, ed., *Philosophical Analysis and History*, pp. 160-92, and W.H. Walsh, 'Colligatory Concepts in History', in W.H. Burston and D. Thompson, eds, *Studies in the Nature and Teaching of History*, London, Routledge & Kegan Paul, 1967, pp. 65-84.

21 'Third Reply to Mr. Goldstein', *British Journal for the Philosophy of Science*, 10: 39, 1959-60, p. 243.

22 'The Principle of Methodological Individualism', p. 187.

23 'Societal Facts', pp. 479ff.

24 Ibid., p. 483.

### Chapter IV    Taylor and the Second World War

1 Penguin Books, 1964, 1961c, containing the Foreword: 'Second Thoughts' (1963). Page numbers in brackets prefaced 'T' in the text above refer to this edition.

2 *Encounter*, 17: 1, 1961, 88-96; reprinted in W.M.R. Louis, ed., *The Origins of the Second World War: A.J.P. Taylor and his Critics*, New York, Wiley, 1972, and in E.M. Robertson, ed., *The Origins of the Second World War*, London, Macmillan, 1971. Page numbers in brackets prefaced 'TR' in the text above refer to the original publication. Other relevant writings of Trevor-Roper include 'The Mind of Adolf Hitler', Introduction to *Hitler's Table Talk, 1941-44*, London, Weidenfeld & Nicolson, 1973, and 'Adolf Hitler', in W. Brockway, ed., *High Moment*, New York, Simon & Schuster, 1955, pp. 231-48.

3 Oxford University Press, 1959.

4 For a rather casual consideration, see Morton White, *Foundations of Historical Knowledge*, New York, Harper & Row, ch. IV; for a more serious but still unfavourable one, see M. Mandelbaum, *The Anatomy of Historical Knowledge*, Johns Hopkins University Press, 1977, ch. IV. A too casual consideration of my own, entitled 'Some Causal Accounts of the American Civil War', in *Daedalus*, summer 1962, pp. 578-92, stands corrected by the present analysis at a number of points.

5 Tr. S. Godman, London, Thames & Hudson, 1955, p. 11. See also D.C. Watt, 'Appeasement: the Rise of the Revisionist School', *Political Quarterly*, 36, 1965, p. 193.

6 *Causation in the Law*, p. 159.

7 It must thus be unlike a case in which a person uses an inappropriate means to accomplish something that comes about anyway: for example, trying to kill someone by magical spells (and 'succeeding'). The case would become less easy to decide if the adoption of the

inappropriate means did, after all, furnish a necessary condition of
the intended result in the particular circumstances, although
accidentally, or in a way not envisaged by the would-be murderer.
Complications of this sort could arise in the literature of the present
dispute, but since I do not see that they do, I ignore them here.

8    Taylor is prepared to apply the same logic to some other agents
who have sometimes been considered causally relevant. Thus he
sets Marxist explanations aside with the following observation:
Before 1939 the great capitalist states, England and America, were
the most anxious to avoid war; and in every country, including
Germany, capitalists were the class most opposed to war' ('T' 137).
As the rest of the present chapter will show, this need not prevent
their achieving causal status on some other paradigm of causality.

9    Besides 'TR' 90–2, see 'Adolf Hitler', pp. 232ff.

10   Besides the critique of Trevor-Roper, see especially P.A. Reynolds,
'Hitler's War?', *History*, 46, 1961, pp. 212ff.; F. Friedel, 'Who
Started the War?', *Reporter*, 26: 2, 1962, p. 52; E. Wiskemann,
review in *Listener*, 65: no. 1673, 1961, p. 707; E.B. Segal, 'A.J.P.
Taylor and History', *Review of Politics*, 26: 4, 1964, pp. 542–3.

11   Review by I.F. Morrow, *International Affairs*, 37: 4, 1961, p. 495.

12   See citation in W.M.R. Louis, *The Origins of the Second World War*,
p. 148.

13   In Ved Mehta, *The Fly and the Fly Bottle*, Boston, Little, Brown,
1962, pp. 175–6, Taylor is reported as saying: 'The difference
between Hughie and me may be no more than that of definition.
If you regard a plan as a great vision, then, of course, Hitler did
have a plan — a lunatic vision. But if you define "plan" as I do, a
plan of day-to-day moves, then Hitler didn't have one.'

14   Taylor goes to quite extraordinary lengths, at times, to show that
Hitler lacked any sort of plan, even for German expansion, let alone
its achievement by a major war. He depicts Hitler as so impulsive
that he decided to annex Austria only at the moment when,
appearing on the balcony at Linz, he was carried away by the
enthusiasm of the crowd ('T' 188), and as so feckless that he dreamed
of settling 100 million Germans in the Ukraine without giving a
thought to what was to be done with the Ukrainians ('T' 139).

15   In fact, in the literature of the dispute whether Hitler intended the
war in the sufficiently strong sense of having a 'plan', three questions
are often run together which I should perhaps have tried to keep
separate: (1) whether Hitler had precise ideas of means to be
employed to achieve his goals; (2) whether he had decided his goals,
and perhaps also his means, long in advance; (3) whether he seriously
intended to implement any plans he may have worked out. Re (2),
Taylor often denies only that Hitler had 'long-range' plans, though
his representing him as utterly impulsive at times may suggest more.

131

Re (3), when confronted by evidence of quite precise planning, Taylor tends to write it off as mere 'contingency' planning. What would German and Italian generals have to talk about when they met, he asks, but war against Britain and France? ('T' 14).

16   'Hitler's War?', p. 217.

17   A.L. Rowse expresses a similar view when he accuses Taylor of confusing questions of strategy and tactics. 'Hitler was flexible as to tactics,' he writes, 'prepared to wait for opportunities to come along and exploit them, but that does not mean that there was not a grand strategy as to which he was inflexible, with an overriding objective: the domination of Europe' (review in *New York Times Book Review*, 7 January 1962, p. 6).

18   'An Apologia for Adolf Hitler', *Commentary*, 33: 2, 1962, p. 183.

19   P.A. Reynolds, 'Hitler's War?', p. 217.

20   For some reservations about what is here called 'conditional willing', see R. Marlin, 'Attempts and the Criminal Law: Three Problems', *Ottawa Law Review,* 8, 1976, pp. 524ff.

21   Actually, there are two different senses in which Hitler might be said to have risked the war, both of which Taylor uses in describing his actions and policies. On the one hand, he might have estimated its probability more or less correctly, and then decided anyway to take a chance. This is the sense which is illustrated by Taylor's report that when Goering, losing his nerve in the final days of the Polish crisis, said to Hitler: 'It is time to stop this *va banque*', Hitler replied: 'It is the only call I ever make' ('T' 305); and again by the declaration of Hitler to his generals a bit earlier: 'We must accept the risk with reckless resolution' – a statement which Trevor-Roper criticizes Taylor for omitting to quote ('TR' 95). On the other hand, like all the statesmen in Taylor's story, Hitler is represented at times as having incurred a risk of war by getting some of the probabilities wrong: that is, he too 'blundered' ('T' 336). It is the assumption that Hitler risked war in the first sense rather than the second, that he took a calculated risk, not just that he miscalculated, that is required by the notion that Hitler conditiónally willed the war.

22   *Causation in the Law,* esp. pp. 30ff. What follows expands upon a briefer account of the same dispute in 'Les explications causales en histoire', *Philosophiques,* 4: 1, 1977, pp. 3–34.

23   The latter half of this paragraph is influenced by the way Trevor-Roper summarizes Taylor's position, which I think is a valid abstraction from it. However, even if it exaggerates what Taylor actually says, Trevor-Roper's summary would be relevant to the analysis of his own concept of cause.

24   Mehta, op. cit., p. 173.

25   Compare S. Gorovitz on relativity to 'classes of comparison' in

'Causal Judgments and Causal Explanations', *Journal of Philosophy*, 62: 2, 1965, pp. 695–711.

26  To cite further examples of Taylor's ascriptions of 'passivity' to Hitler and 'activity' to his enemies: we are told that Hitler 'did not "seize" power. He waited for it to be thrust upon him . . .' ('T' 101). On the other hand, the British 'took the lead in dismantling Czechoslovakia' ('T' 8). Taylor scarcely grants a genuine initiative to Hitler before the approach to Russia in 1939 ('T' 314).

27  It was the same in the case of Memel: the problem 'exploded of itself' ('T' 258). Hitler had 'restrained' the German population there as best he could, but 'the German occupation of Prague flung the people of Memel into ungovernable excitement; there was no longer any holding them' ('T' 257). Taylor carries this account of a merely responding Hitler into the war itself. The invasion of Belgium and Holland on 10 May 1940, he says, was purely 'a defensive move: to secure the Ruhr from Allied invasion. The conquest of France was an unforeseen bonus' ('T' 19).

28  'Hitler's War?', p. 215.

29  'An Apologia for Adolf Hitler', p. 183.

30  A further striking example is Taylor's reporting that, in the late spring of 1939, Hitler finally 'allowed' the German press to write about the German minority in Poland, 'to ease things along as he supposed' ('T' 259). As Reynolds observes, this is 'a remarkable euphemism' for 'the flood of vituperation' which then poured forth (op. cit., p. 214).

31  A number of Taylor's critics have thought it relevant to argue along similar lines. Thus E.B. Segal writes: 'By reducing all activism in German policy to the lowest point possible, Taylor has paradoxically reversed the ordinary chain of causal explanation. Hitler's bold enterprises have become simply reactions to British and French moves; and what were in part their responses to positive German steps have been transformed into active initiatives which dropped concessions into Hitler's lap'. This is more than a misuse of evidence, Segal complains; it is 'a failure of conception' ('A.J.P. Taylor and History', p. 542). T.W. Mason and A.L. Rowse make much the same response. Rejecting Taylor's account of who was a problem to whom, Mason observes that 'in a longer perspective, the initiatives of other governments appear rather as responses to problems raised by Nazi Germany. Crucial decisions were certainly made in all the capitals of Europe, but the Third Reich determined what it was that the victor powers had to decide about.' ('Some Origins of the Second World War', reprinted in Robertson, op. cit., p. 110). A.L. Rowse sees Taylor as 'putting the cart before the horse'. The cause of the war, he says, was not 'Allied dithering', but 'Hitler's dynamic drive towards world power – to which Britain and France were merely reacting

insufficiently strongly' (*New York Times Book Review*, 7 January 1962, p. 6).

32 Taylor's mode of argument here appears similar to that found in certain legal cases by Hart and Honoré (op. cit., pp. 55, 76, 179). The considerations which may enter such cases are very complicated, and are indicated only roughly above.

33 Others who 'pushed' were von Papen ('T' 181) and Daladier ('T' 220).

34 London, Hamilton, 1952, ch. 2.

35 It is possible that, in *Origins*, Taylor confuses the question of value-freedom with that of 'detachment' ('T' 29). If by the latter is meant not being guided by some ulterior purpose (such as a political goal in the present), it is easy to agree with Taylor about what the historian's obligation is *qua* historian (and indeed to sympathize with his response to the charge that he has given comfort to neo-Nazis: that this is 'a disgraceful argument to be used against a work of history' ('T' 8). However, many of Taylor's critics have in fact questioned his detachment in this sense — see, for example, Trevor-Roper ('TR' 96) and Segal (op. cit., pp. 544–5).

36 A moral dimension may have to be recognized even in the first paradigm, if the notion of conditional willing is allowed, and extended to the case where something is merely risked: for the question may arise whether the envisaged risk was great enough to warrant the causal attribution, and the answer to that may vary with the moral circumstances.

37 Compare the end of chapter III, section IV.

38 For example, T.W. Mason complains that Taylor ignores 'the profoundest cause of the Second World War . . . the distinctive character and role of National Socialism', with its 'expansionist drive' and lack of any concept of 'an ultimate *status quo*' (Robertson, op. cit., pp. 106, 108.

39 Mehta, op. cit., p. 173.

40 'A.J.P. Taylor and History', p. 536.

41 Review article, *Historical Journal*, 4: 2, 1961, p. 224.

42 Op. cit., pp. 227–8. It is of interest to find an historian here answering Watkins's question (chapter III, section IV above) whether individual human beings can be causes (or, at any rate, *when* they can be causes) on quasi-moral grounds.

43 Op. cit., pp. 224–5.

44 Collingwood attempts something of the sort, although with limited success, for three 'senses' of cause that he recognizes in his *An Essay on Metaphysics*, Clarendon Press, 1940, pp. 291–2.

45 In an evocative passage, Hexter has represented this requirement as a general obligation laid upon the historian. He first quotes with approval the following remarks of Garrett Mattingly about the Duke

of Medina Sidonia, admiral of the ill-fated Spanish Armada: 'There is a tendency of late to speak more kindly of Medina Sidonia . . . to recognize his courage and his administrative ability . . . Not that such a judgment would have been much comfort to Medina Sidonia. Whatever he did, it was not enough. Nor does it matter at all to the dead whether they receive justice at the hands of succeeding generations. But to the living to do justice, however belatedly, should matter.' Hexter adds the observation: 'To Garrett Mattingly it was important to do justice to the Duke Medina Sidonia almost four centuries after the Armada disaster, because Medina Sidonia was a man he humanly encountered in the record of the past. Not to be concerned with justice to one or many so encountered is to diminish, not their human nature, but ours. And so "to the living to do justice, however belatedly, should matter".' *Proceedings of the XIII International Congress of Historical Sciences,* Moscow, Nauka Publishing House, 1970, pp. 31–2.

46  *The Anatomy of Historical Knowledge,* pp. 90–3.

## Chapter V    Spengler and the Life-Cycle of Cultures

1  *Outline of History,* London, Cassell, 1920.
2  *The Rise of the West,* University of Chicago Press, 1963.
3  *A Study of History,* Oxford University Press, 1934–54.
4  Tr. C.F. Atkinson, London, Allen & Unwin, 1926, 1928; originally published in German in 1918 and 1922 (first volume revised in 1923). Page numbers in brackets in the text above refer to the one-volume edition of the English translation published in 1932.
5  See, for example, H.N. Frye, 'Toynbee and Spengler', *Canadian Forum,* 27: 319, 1947, p. 111. For Spengler's relation to Fascism see also B. Mazlish, *The Riddle of History,* London, Harper & Row, 1966, p. 318, and H.S. Hughes, *Oswald Spengler: a Critical Estimate,* New York, Scribner, 1952, p. 124.
6  Hughes, op. cit., p. 66.
7  This timeliness was to a large extent accidental, since Spengler's views had been worked out before the outbreak of the war. Like Toynbee, who relates how his interpretation of history came to him suddenly while reading Thucydides' *History of the Peloponnesian War* and seeing parallels with trends in his own society, Spengler claims to have had an 'illumination', in this case stimulated by the Moroccan crisis of 1911, which brought France and Germany to the brink of hostilities. Spengler claims not only to have seen the world war approaching, but to have seen it as a pre-ordained 'change of phase' in a 'great historical organization' (I, 46–7).
8  'Oswald Spengler', in *Architects of Modern Thought,* Toronto,

CBC Publications, 1955, p. 87; and '*The Decline of the West* by Oswald Spengler', *Daedalus*, 103: 1, 1974, p. 112.

9  'Two Wrestlers with the Angel', in his *Dutch Civilization in the Seventeenth Century and other Essays,* London, Collins, 1968, p. 160.

10  Op. cit., p. 7.

11  See his *The Philosophy of History,* tr. C.J. Friedrich, New York, Dover, 1956.

12  In the face of this question, Spengler's biological analogy already, in fact, begins to show strain, since for some purposes he treats cultures as similar members of a single species, whereas for others (for example, when he wishes to emphasize cultural uniqueness) he treats them as if they were single existing members of different species. This induces A.L. Kroeber to remark that 'the actual parallel to Spengler's view of culture would be a biological world in which [there would be only] a hen, an eagle, a squirrel, a basilisk, plus one individual each of perhaps a half-dozen other species'. *Style and Civilizations,* Cornell University Press, 1957, p. 97.

13  See, for example, J.T. Shotwell, 'Spengler', in *Essays in Intellectual History Dedicated to James Harvey Robinson,* Freeport, N.Y., Books for Libraries Press, 1968, 1929c, p. 65. Frye notes that five of Spengler's cultures, the Egyptian, Classical, Magian, Western and Russian, do in fact run roughly in sequence ('*The Decline of the West*', p. 5), but for Spengler, this can be no more than an accident, without theoretical importance.

14  Spengler enlarges on the point: 'In the world-consciousness of the Hellenes all experience, not merely the personal but the common past, was immediately transmuted into a timeless, immobile, mythically-fashioned background for the particular momentary present; thus the history of Alexander the Great began even before his death to be merged by Classical sentiment in the Dionysus legend, and to Caesar there seemed at the least nothing preposterous in claiming descent from Venus' (I, 8).

15  It is very different, too, from that spiritual rebirth and cultural renaissance that Toynbee claims to find in the religious experiences of the 'penalized' classes of a disintegrating civilization, although he has been thought to have been inspired by Spengler's views in this connection. See, for example, P.A. Sorokin, *Modern Historical and Social Philosophies,* New York, Dover, 1963, p. 111.

16  The word is Frye's in '*The Decline of the West*', p. 6. Hughes says of Spengler: 'The strength of his perspective on history lies in its imaginative imprecision', op. cit., p. 74. The Tables, he says, were a mistake. But these, surely are of the essence of what Spengler is doing, at any rate at the first of the two 'empirical' levels distinguished in section VIII below.

17  *A Study of History*, vol. VI, p. 321.

18  This is presumably what he has in mind when he says that, while causality is rigorously deterministic, destiny is not (I, 118, 145). Spengler denies that he is a determinist.

19  Like most of those who assert, or come close to asserting, determinism at the social level (whether called this or not) while allowing a high degree of freedom at the individual level (see chapter IV, section VI, for another case), Spengler does not ask how these apparently discordant doctrines are to be reconciled; for that would be to involve himself in the problem of 'analysis' (see below).

20  'Oswald Spengler and the Theory of Historical Cycles', in his *Essays in the Philosophy of History*, ed. W. Debbins, University of Texas Press, 1965, p. 69.

21  For a salutary protest against philosophers' 'obsession' with the question 'why?', see J.H. Hexter, *The History Primer*, New York, Basic Books, 1971, p. 199.

22  *The Disinherited Mind*, London, Meridian, 1959, p. 182.

23  '*The Decline of the West*', p. 7. Rather surprisingly, however, Frye seems to deny that ageing, both as Spengler understands it and as he is prepared to accept the idea himself, involves change of value, at any rate during the pre-civilization period. As Western art develops, he says (in explanation of Spengler), it is 'not getting better or worse; it is simply getting older' ('Toynbee and Spengler', p. 112). On the other hand, when he wishes to support Spengler's view that our own society is approaching old age, he says, with obviously evaluative overtones, that we cannot 'pretend' that such things as 'the violence and overcrowding of our almost unmanageable cities', or 'the brutality and vacuousness of our standard forms of entertainment' are not 'features of cultural aging' ('*Decline of the West*', p. 13). It is difficult to see that Spengler was not making similar judgments of value when he represented various late summer phenomena as 'mature' in the sense of reaching the high point of creative achievement.

24  Op. cit., p. 70.

25  Spengler sometimes denies that, in history, it is understanding we are looking for at all, understanding being associated with causal analysis (II, 266). But he makes no attempt to hew to this eccentric position, and I ignore it in formulating his views.

26  In view of this, it must be acknowledged that my second large question (in section II): 'What is the productive mechanism of history?', may seem, when addressed to Spengler, rather unhappily phrased. In his notion of 'destiny', he nevertheless offers an answer to the related, and perhaps appropriately vaguer question: 'What is the ultimate explanation of history's assuming the pattern it does?'

27  Spengler nevertheless allows himself, at one point, to entertain the possibility that the very style of a culture may arise from physical

causes: 'In some mysterious fashion, the Euclidean existence is linked with the multitude of little islands and promontories of the Aegean, and the passionate Western roving in the infinite with the broad plains of Franconia and Burgundy and Saxony' (I, 203). This, however, appears to be an uncharacteristic lapse.

28  'Oswald Spengler and the Theory of Historical Cycles', pp. 67, 71. Spengler does, at one point, say that a particular culture is '*acquired* in so far that every individual soul re-enacts for itself that creative act [attributed in a primary sense to the culture itself] and unfolds in early childhood the symbol of depth to which its existence is predestined' (I, 174). But this incipient Collingwoodianism is not developed.

29  To the extent that he does this, he would be an 'historicist' in the sense made current by K.R. Popper's *The Poverty of Historicism*, London, Routledge & Kegan Paul, 1957. That is, he would extrapolate allegedly perceived trends of individual developments.

30  *Style and Civilizations*, p. 89, n. 2.

31  It is amusing, in this connection, to find Toynbee accepting with gratitude the opinion of a reviewer that a close reading of his *Study of History* shows him, too, to be 'a Magian soul born out of his time'. 'Toynbee's whole adult life', writes F.H. Underhill, 'has been spent in a long struggle by his subconscious Magian self to overcome the Hellenic education imposed on his conscious English self at school and college.' *A Study of History*, vol. XII, pp. 670–1, n. 3.

32  'Two Wrestlers', p. 169.

33  '*The Decline of the West*', p. 10.

34  'Oswald Spengler and the Theory of Historical Cycles', p. 62; *The Idea of History*, Clarendon Press, 1946, p. 183.

35  Op. cit., p. 69.

36  p. 241.

37  Spengler sometimes appears on the verge of extending his isolation thesis beyond cultures to smaller groups like nations and classes (which also have 'souls'). For example, he denies that Athens and Sparta, or England, Germany and France really understand each other (II, 171); and in Faustian culture, at least, he doubts that a diplomat can understand a craftsman, or a workman a peasant (II, 29). Since, for him, history is lived by elites, the latter may not present a serious problem for his theory; but the former would threaten it with still another dimension of incoherence.

38  This difficulty in Spengler was pointed out to me by Mr Axel Harvey.

39  To illustrate the point further, one might suggest, only half-facetiously, the following sort of test of skill for a would-be Spenglerian historian. He should be presented with a pack of cards representing, on their faces, the remains of a number of cultures previously unknown to him — buildings, paintings, poems, town

plans, weapons, types of dress, and the like — each card having the correct date printed on the reverse side. He should then be asked to sort the pack face up, first by 'style' into different cultures, and then again, for each cultural pile, by 'age' — that is, by apparent 'freshness' or 'tiredness'. How good his 'physiognomic tact' really was would be shown on turning over the cards, which should now be in chronological order.

# Index